From Ice Set Free

By Bruce Clements

TWO AGAINST THE TIDE

THE FACE OF ABRAHAM CANDLE

FROM ICE SET FREE

Bruce Clements

FROM ICE
SET FREE

The Story of Otto Kiep

Farrar, Straus and Giroux

NEW YORK

FIRST PRINTING, 1972

Published simultaneously in Canada by Doubleday Canada Ltd., Toronto
Printed in the United States of America
Designed by Herb Johnson

112884

THIS BOOK IS DEDICATED TO A GOOD WOMAN,

Hanna Kiep

Contents

From Ice Set Free

Langfier Ltd, Glasgow

I

A Glasgow Family

Otto Carl Kiep was born in Saltcoats, Scotland, in July 1886, and died by hanging in Berlin, Germany, in August 1944. He was never famous, and hardly anyone now remembers his name, but he was a very special kind of man—strong, gentle, intelligent, and deeply honest, with a wild and funny imagination. It was his honesty which led to his death. He refused to tell lies to his friends at a time when telling the truth was a crime.

There are some men about whom you can say, "Because I know him, I also know his world and his time." Otto Kiep is such a man. He is a mirror of the first half of this century, showing the best of its hopes, the clearest of its thinking, the brightest and darkest of its days.

He grew up in Glasgow, where his father and uncle had a timber-importing business. There is a picture, taken in 1899, which shows him with his three brothers and his young sister, Ida. Each of the boys is dressed according to his place in the family. Klaus, the oldest, has a high collar, a vest, a wide tie with a pearl pin, a watch chain, and a handkerchief. Louis, the next, has a high collar, a vest, a *narrow* tie with a pearl pin, and a watch chain, but no handkerchief. Otto, number three, has a high collar, a vest, and a narrow tie, but no pearl pin, no handkerchief, and probably no watch chain, though that may be hidden behind Ida's left shoulder. Max, the youngest son, has a turned-down collar, no vest, no watch chain or handkerchief, and a plaid, little-boy necktie.

Klaus, Louis, Otto, and Max all look neat. Ida looks sloppy, with her hair pulled back from her forehead and pushed around behind her ears. Her mother was against prettiness. Wanting to look pretty, she thought, was immoral. The only one in the family who cared how Ida looked was Otto. He would buy her hair ribbons, make sure she had something special to wear on Easter Sunday, and tell her stories about a princess named "Ida the Beautiful." ("Now this is a true story," he would say before he began. "Will you believe me?" And she would answer, "Honor bright, every word.")

The Kieps were Germans, and glad and proud of it. The children's notebooks and pencils and rulers came from Hamburg, and so did the whole family's underwear, and on January 27 every year they celebrated Kaiser Wilhelm II's birthday by eating a big *Baisertorte* from Sautermeister's Bakery and drinking good German wine. Even Ida got a glass. Mrs. Kiep belonged to the German Women's Union for Colonial Care, and Mr. Kiep, who in addition to running a timber business was the Imperial German Consul for Glasgow and Western Scotland, started a German-language church in Glasgow, even though he didn't believe in God. There was already one German church in the city, but it had a congregation full of working-class immigrants whose children were going to become British, and he would have nothing to do with it.

"Serve German trade and you serve Germany," the Consul would sometimes say as they sat at the dinner table, or went for their Sunday walk, or took a sailboat across the Clyde River on a summer evening. Klaus and Louis were going to serve German trade by joining the fleet, Klaus as a naval engineer and Louis as a ship's officer. Otto was supposed to serve it by coming into the timber business. To his father's way of thinking, Otto was perfect for it—intelligent, hard-working, careful—a born businessman, ready to out-think and out-work the British.

Otto had a different idea. He wanted to serve the German government, "to be like Bismarck," to stand for the good character of the German people—their enthusiasm, their honesty, their sense of duty, their self-respect, and their generosity—to help Germany become what he knew she ought to become, the spiritual and political center of Europe.

But he couldn't fight his father. It was part of his training, part of his faith, that a father required obedience. Louis might be able to figure out how to obey his father and still, somehow, get his own way, but Otto couldn't. Obedience, simply and directly understood, was what his conscience needed. Besides, what right did he have to oppose his father? Johannes Kiep was a man of the world, over fifty years old. He knew what was happening everywhere. He belonged to the Royal Clyde Yacht Club. He had opinions about things, and good reasons for them. He was honest and he was strong, and Otto feared him with a kind of moral fear. So, when anyone asked him what he was going to do when he grew up, he always said that he expected to go into the timber business with his father and his uncle.

And he would have done it, too, if it hadn't been for Dr. Karl Wichmann, who came to live in his house and changed the direction of his life.

II

Ambitions

Karl Wichmann came from Westphalia. He was five feet seven inches tall, with a homely face, clear blue eyes, and narrow shoulders. He arrived at the Kiep house in November 1898 to tutor Klaus and Louis and get them ready to transfer to German schools. He had just won a doctoral degree in history, and he wanted to see the British Isles, and perhaps teach in a British university, before settling down in Germany. He wore English-style clothes and had a small moustache, which he had grown to make himself look older. He always leaned forward when someone asked him a question, and hesitated a few seconds before answering, which made some people think he was very stupid and other people think he was very wise. He spoke English slowly and clearly, with an Oxford accent, and he loved old books. His favorite sport was hunting in second-hand bookstores.

He had a wonderful book collection, including a leather-bound edition of Shakespeare, in perfect condition, printed in 1767.

He arrived at noon on a rainy Saturday, after sitting up all night on the train from London. Mr. Kiep met him at the door—which was something he didn't do for everybody—and led him into the dining room for marrow dumpling soup, lamb chops, potatoes, green beans, and fruit compote. (The Kieps were great eaters, and hated to be away from good food.) The whole family was there, including Ida, who sat between Otto and Max on one side of the table. Dr. Wichmann sat on the other side, with Klaus on his right and Louis on his left. The Consul and Mrs. Kiep sat at either end.

Otto was twelve years old then, and beginning to see that his mother and father didn't like each other. They respected each other's abilities, and they believed in each other's powers, but they left each other alone most of the time, and they almost never talked freely or laughed together. As soon as the soup came, Mrs. Kiep began to ask Dr. Wichmann questions, trying to find out what kind of man he was. Wichmann, leaning forward, gave her his whole attention, and everyone else just ate and listened.

They talked first about German students. Mrs. Kiep wanted to know if they were as *serious* as they ought to be, if enough of them wanted to serve their country. "Over here," she said, "the universities make gentlemen, which is enough for the British, perhaps, but certainly not for us."

Wichmann hesitated a moment. "They make interesting gentlemen, I think."

"They can afford it. Let them go their own way. The British are different, Dr. Wichmann. They have less self-respect than we do, and they're not so ready to do their duty. I grew up here, and went to school here. The

British as a people *enjoy* being amateurs. They do not understand Germans, as a rule."

Dr. Wichmann asked if the Kaiser's decision to increase the size of the German navy had changed British feelings. Mrs. Kiep shook her head. No, British feelings were *fixed*. They had always looked down upon Germans, in their special British way, and they always would.

They talked about patriotism. The German nation was so young—not yet thirty years old—and every German needed to be a patriot. Wichmann talked a few minutes about Bismarck and his place in the history of Germany and Europe, and Mrs. Kiep sat listening with a peaceful look on her face. She wanted to like people and to believe in them. Weak men worried her, and dishonest men made her hard, but an honest, strong man always made her happy, especially when she agreed with what he was saying. She smiled and changed the subject.

"Do you swim?"

"No, dear lady, I don't."

"Then you must learn. Everyone should know how to swim. Klaus will teach you. He was my best pupil."

"You taught your children to swim?"

"All except Ida, who will learn next year. Swimming is quite simple, once you overcome your fear of water. Everyone can float, even Westphalians."

Otto had been watching Wichmann carefully, and now decided what he looked like: a small giraffe with blue eyes. No, a small *intelligent* giraffe with blue eyes and a moustache.

The boys kept eating. Dr. Wichmann began to relax and talk more. Along with the English language he had somehow picked up the English habit of treating serious things in an unserious way, without mocking them. It was a habit Otto had, too, and would keep all his life.

"You admire the British, don't you?" Mrs. Kiep said.

"Yes, I do," Wichmann said. "They don't insist on *understanding* everything."

Dessert was finished, and Mr. Kiep leaned back in his chair and looked around the table. "This afternoon," he said, "Klaus will go over his financial accounts with me, Louis will pump out the well house, Otto will take Dr. Wichmann for a walk, during which they will speak German only, and Max will ask his mother how he may help her. If she has nothing for him to do, he will work on his Latin. Ida may play in her room or look at a book." He looked at Dr. Wichmann and smiled. "When you are settled, before you and Otto begin your walk, perhaps you will come into the library and we can begin to become acquainted."

Otto left the house with Dr. Wichmann a little before three. His plan was to take him down the Great Western Road as far as the center of the city, come back along St. Vincent's Street past his father's office, and then walk down to the big shed on the Clyde River where the Kiep timber was unloaded and stored. Halfway to the center of the city he thought of something else. "Would you like to see an old friend of ours? She's lived in Glasgow all her life."

"Yes."

"She used to be our washerwoman, but now she's too old. Her name's Margaret McCann."

They turned right and Otto started zigzagging toward the river, one street down, one alley across, the next street down. The streets were full of people—small, filthy children, twelve- and thirteen-year-old boys with hands and faces black from the foundry, young men and women with the eyes of old people, and drunks of all ages. A few blocks from the river two tall boys in tail coats ran by them, lucky apprentice clerks in some fancy downtown store.

They went down an alley with high, rough stone walls on both sides. "Do they have streets like this in Hamburg?" Otto asked. Wichmann shook his head and they both stepped against a wall to let a boy who was drunk go by. "German working men don't look like these people, either. Your mother is absolutely right. The German worker has more self-respect. He believes in what he's doing. These people don't."

After two more zigzags, they came to the building where "Old Maggie" McCann lived, and Otto led the way inside. They walked up a dark flight of worn stone stairs, turned right, and walked up another flight. The place stank, and he was suddenly sorry that he had brought Wichmann here. He didn't want to show Maggie to somebody who would be disgusted by her. After all, she was a good, clean woman, with a good heart. He hoped she wouldn't be home.

He knocked on her door, and she opened it right away. She was a tall old woman, with large, tired eyes, and not many teeth in her mouth. Still, there was something lively and almost young about her.

"Master Otto. Good Saturday to you. And to you, sir."

Otto introduced Dr. Wichmann, she invited them inside, brought them to wooden chairs near the window, went across the room, and made tea. She apologized when she served it, because her cups didn't match. After the health of everyone at the Kiep house was asked about, she turned to Dr. Wichmann. "And, Doctor," she said, "what brings you to Glasgow?"

He told her that he had wanted to visit Great Britain for a long time, and considered himself very fortunate now to be able to be with the Consul and his wife and their children. Then he talked about his trip across the English Channel to Dover, during which he was seasick, and his feelings as a foreigner on his first sight of Glasgow. He talked to her as he might have talked to the mother of the girl he wanted to marry—hopefully and seriously.

He asked her about Glasgow, and she told him how the city used to be before the electric trolleys and the "new trade" came. Her great-grandmother had lived in Glasgow before the factories, she said, and could remember whole weeks of clear skies. Wichmann nodded. "Country air is the only air," he said.

They drank tea and talked for over an hour, and when Otto finally led Wichmann back down on the street, he felt as if he had known the man for years, as if they had gone up and down hundreds of smelly staircases together.

They went down to the river to look at the Kiep timber shed. Otto always enjoyed going there, partly because he liked the smell of wood and water mixed, and partly because it belonged to his family. It was, in some sense, *his* shed. Sometimes, when he was there, he could imagine himself taking over the business and liking it.

Everywhere there were bins and hills of wood—firewood, wood for paving streets, furniture and flooring wood, boards and blocks and slats of red, white, yellow, and pitch pine, birch, ash, mahogany, and poplar, all brought together by his father, who sent the orders, set the prices, kept up the standards, paid the employees, and made sure that the wood came on time and was shipped on time.

It was after five o'clock, so he tried to tell Wichmann everything he knew about the business in ten minutes. He succeeded.

On the way home Wichmann did most of the talking. He had just spent five days walking over London, and he talked about the differences between it and Berlin. Otto listened and asked questions because he wanted to be polite, but he wasn't really thinking about what the man was saying. He was thinking about the man himself. It was as if he had just gotten a new brother.

After supper that night the family started talking about Klaus's future, and Otto told his vision of how it was going to be. "Klaus is going to be the most talented ship-engine builder in the world," he said. "By the time he's twenty-five he'll be world-famous. He'll walk from ship to ship in Hamburg, and climb down inside them, and screw in new pipes and nuts and bolts, and take out the old boilers and put in new ones, some shaped like doughnuts and some shaped like crown muffins and some shaped like currant cakes—which will be his favorite kind of boilers—and a few shaped like ordinary boilers. And when he's through with a ship—each job will take him about two days—he'll polish up the propeller and climb out into the daylight again and go on to the next ship. And every ship he works on will go twice as fast as it did before, and ships will line up in the harbor waiting for him to put in his cake-shaped boilers and polish up their propellers with his special propeller polish. He'll be the only man in the history of the world who ever walked across the Atlantic Ocean. He'll walk from ship to ship, all the way from Hamburg to New York, and make them all go twice as fast as before, and never get his feet wet. And when he gets to New York and walks across the wharf there'll be this terrible clanking sound, because his feet will have turned to iron from all those ships, but he won't mind because his wife, a former steelworker from Bremen, will be able to scrape the rust off his feet and paint them every week. The only trouble is, he won't be able to swim any more. And he'll live to be a hundred years old and die from eating bad oysters."

By the time he was through, everybody was laughing, Mrs. Kiep louder than anyone. "Oh, Otto," she said, "you and your wild imagination."

Otto shook his head. "It's not my imagination. It's really going to be that way."

He had such a serious expression on his face that they all started laughing again, and after a few moments he shrugged and started laughing too.

The fact is that in some sense Otto really believed all his stories. When he looked at Klaus and told him he would soon be the greatest ship's engineer in the world, he was giving a form to Klaus's secret ambition, holding up a mirror to him and saying, in a slightly crazy way, that he believed in him. When he told Max that he would some day become Mayor of the Village of Lower Apolda—"shortly before its merger with Upper Apolda to form Great Apolda"—and get so fat his chain of office wouldn't fit around him, and have so many children he would have to give them numbers instead of names, he was not only having fun, he was also telling Max to be careful or he might grow up to be a fat, smug fool. And when he told his sister stories about "Princess Ida," he was helping her to see an ideal, and saying that he already saw in her the beautiful and good woman she was going to become.

Late that evening, when everyone else had gone to bed, Mrs. Kiep and Wichmann sat in the drawing room with glasses of wine and talked about her male children. Wichmann liked Klaus a lot, and said so. There was something *free* about him. He was a person who would live his own life without a lot of foolish pride. He didn't say much about Louis, because children who talked like successful grownups made him nervous. Otto, he thought, was very special. "He's like clear water," he said.

Mrs. Kiep looked directly at him. "He has a noble spirit," she said. "I hope you will do what you can for him. He should go to the university, and he won't unless his father changes his mind. Otto is the best of my children, Dr. Wichmann, and one should help him."

Dr. Wichmann was amazed that she would say this to a stranger in such a clear, straight-out way. "I'll do whatever I can," he said.

"Good."

III

Ilfeld

Oᴛᴛᴏ was confirmed as a member of the Protestant Church by Pastor Reinhold Münchmeyer on Palm Sunday, 1900, in the chapel of the Christian Institute on Bothwell Street. He had received instruction twice a week for two years, and knew Luther's *Small Catechism,* both the questions and the answers, by heart.

There were two things about Christianity that fascinated and moved him. One was the character of Christ— tough-minded, persistent, and honest—telling the truth no matter what the cost. The other was the idea of *creation by the word.* God said the word "light," and there was light. God said "earth," and the earth suddenly, in that moment, appeared. That was the kind of power Otto had been born believing in.

As he took the vow to be Christ's true disciple all the days of his life, God being his helper, he felt serious and lighthearted at the same time. Christian faith was a good thing in a world full of good things. It was, perhaps, the *best* thing in a world full of good things, better than sunshine and music and honor and sailing and work. It proved that life was more powerful than death. The fact that the Consul thought it was a stupid religion didn't bother him at all. His father was now sitting in the front row with a satisfied look on his face, proving that even atheists needed Christianity once in a while.

Nine days later, on April 17, 1900, Otto left Scotland with his mother to enroll in the Cloisterschool in Ilfeld. The Consul had been against his going, but during a vacation cruise the previous summer Wichmann had persuaded him to change his mind. They were sailing at night in the open water south of the Isle of Mull between Oban and Iona. It was a beautiful evening, the sky was full of stars, the boys were playing cards in the main cabin and the two men were relaxing over brandy and cigars on the afterdeck.

"Otto would like to go to Ilfeld next spring," Wichmann said.

"I know. I am not for it. I have other plans for him."

"I think he would do as well as Louis is doing," Wichmann said, "and of course the Cloisterschool is excellent preparation for the university."

"Do you see Otto as a scholar?"

Wichmann shook his head. "Klaus is your scholar."

The Consul looked surprised, but didn't say anything.

Wichmann took a sip of his brandy. "Otto has a more practical mind. He wants to organize things and change them."

The Consul remained quiet. He had never thought of Otto as a *political man* before, and the idea pleased him.

"What would he study at the university?"

"Law. He's very interested in government and international trade, just as you are."

"I'll consider it."

Wichmann never mentioned the matter again, but a few weeks later the Consul wrote a letter to Ilfeld requesting a place for Otto. One thing he made clear to him, however. When he was done at Ilfeld, he would have to spend at least nine months as an apprentice in the office of Carl Kiep and Brother, Glasgow, before he did anything else.

So Wichmann got, with no extra pay, an extra student. He immediately gave Otto an oral examination, and decided that he needed work in German history and literature. He brought him a dozen history books, an atlas, and a volume of *Essays on German Culture*. Starting on the first of October they worked together from seven to nine every evening. By the end of December they were ready for European geography and Goethe's *Faust*.

Otto knew *Faust* already, but reading it with Wichmann made it a completely different work. He learned hundreds of lines by heart, and on Easter Sunday afternoon, 1900, as they walked along the bank of the Clyde, they could recite together Faust's speech about the meaning of spring and Easter:

> *From ice set free are brooks and river*
> *Touched by spring's fair, life-giving glance,*
> *And in the valley new hope blooms.*
> *Winter, old and weakened,*
> *Has withdrawn to wild mountaintops.*
> *Still in flight, he sends from there*
> *Impotent showers of grainy ice,*
> *White ribbons, across the greening fields.*
> *The sun, however, permits no white.*
> *Everything is moving, reaching and forming,*

Trying to come alive with colors.
People in their Sunday best
Provide the flowers missing on the scene.
Turn about upon these heights
And look back onto the town!
From the dark and hollow gate
Pushes and flows a colorful crowd.
All of them want to catch some sun.
They celebrate the Lord's resurrection,
For they themselves have just arisen . . .

It was hard for him to leave Glasgow because of Ida. The day before he went he took her for a walk, bought her muffins and cocoa in a tea shop, and came home the long way by trolley. He promised to write her a letter on the first of every month as long as he was away. On the day he left she stood on the dock crying and waving so hard that Otto, standing with his mother at the rail of the boat and waving back, almost cried himself.

They visited some friends of Mrs. Kiep in Altona on Wednesday, stayed overnight in Magdeburg on Thursday, and arrived in Ilfeld a little before noon on Friday. Louis met them at the station, and they had lunch in a small restaurant across the street. Then Mrs. Kiep got a porter with a cart for Otto's trunk, and they started along the gently curving main street, past stores, houses, and gardens, toward the school. Near the end of town was an enormous estate yard closed off from the street by a high stone fence and a large wooden gate. Two hundred meters farther on was the church, and next to the church, facing a small grass park, was the old cloister building where monks had once lived and where now a few teachers and their families had apartments. Just beyond that was the school.

It was bigger than Otto had expected, a gray stone building three stories high, with a long row of wide windows across the first floor, a triple-arched entrance, and a steep, overhanging, red tile roof. As they walked toward it, Otto thought back to the Hillhead School, which suddenly seemed very small and amateurish. He suddenly wished he was back there. Walking down the wide hall toward the principal's office, he even began to doubt Wichmann, who had said he was ready. What did Wichmann know about the kinds of tests a German boarding school might give an entering student from Scotland? Even an English exam here might have things on it that he'd never heard of. Louis had passed all his entrance examinations the year before, but that didn't mean anything. *Of course* Louis had passed his exams. Louis *always* passed things. He knew how.

Fifteen minutes later, after a quick meeting with Dr. Rudolf Mücke, the principal, Otto was trying to write a Latin examination in an empty classroom facing the street. He was in a panic. He couldn't remember verb forms he had known for years. An hour later the same thing was happening in a Greek exam. Geometry was a little better, and he did his English in less than half an hour, but at five, when the Primus—the number-one student—of the Obersekunda class picked up his papers, he knew for the first time in his life how it felt to fail in school.

He and Louis and his mother had dinner together at the Tanne Inn, and he spent the night with Louis in the

room they were to share, number 23 at the end of the
stone walk near the old chapel. (Kurt Böcking, the third
student in number 23, was still away for the Easter holidays and would be back on Sunday.) Before they went to
sleep, Louis tried to cheer him up about the exams and
make him feel at home. "There are 162 students here,
and at least half of them failed one of the entrance
exams," he said. It didn't help. The next morning at nine
he met with Principal Mücke and his mother in the
principal's office.

"You know, certainly," the principal said, looking directly at him, "that you did not do well in either the
Latin or the Greek. The geometry was satisfactory, and
naturally, the English was excellent, perfect. The Latin
and Greek, however, are fundamental."

Mrs. Kiep assured him that Otto was a top student in
both languages, and Mücke listened respectfully, nodding two or three times, looking at Otto, judging him.

"I have every confidence that you are right," he said
finally. "Nevertheless, we will only be able to admit him
to the Obertertia class on probation. If it should prove
necessary, we will move him to the Untertertia without
delay. We cannot keep him in a class for which he is not
prepared."

Otto listened, trying not to let his face show the shame
he felt at being admitted "on probation." He was sorry
he had ever wanted to come.

From that moment on, he thought of Mücke as "the
Judge," the man who decided who would go and who
would stay. Later that spring the principal expelled two
princes, Jost-Christian von Hammerstein, prince of

Stolberg-Rossla, whose father was Prussian Minister of the Interior, and the Prince von Bockum-Dolffs, Jost's dear friend and roommate, because they had gone out after curfew to drink and dance with the local girls at the Firemen's Ball. They were minor princes from small places, but they were still princes, and when they were expelled together, everyone was shocked. Some students said that Mücke had private reasons for getting rid of them, but Otto was sure he didn't. They had broken the curfew, that's all, and princes or not, they had to go.

Mrs. Kiep's train left at two on Saturday, and after seeing her off, he went for a walk alone. It was a bright, almost cold afternoon, but the sweet smell of spring was coming out of the woods and across the fields.

"From ice set free . . ."

He tried to picture his mother on the Magdeburg train, but instead he saw her sitting at her end of the dining-room table counting out grapes as she had the Sunday before he left, twelve for each of the boys and eight for Ida.

He walked faster. All of a sudden the trees and the road started swimming in front of his eyes. He felt helpless. He had been so sure that he wanted to come to Germany, to be in a school where the history teachers didn't call Bismarck "a middle-European politician," or say that Germany was "a danger to Europe." Germany was beautiful and orderly, the German people were moral and kind and sincere, and almost everything was just as he had expected it to be, but still he wanted to go home to where his house was, and eat at his table, and smell the Clyde again.

He kept walking, with his back straight and his eyes forward, until the crying was over. He took a deep breath. He wished it was night, because he was tired. He went down to a narrow stream next to the road and splashed water on his face and then dried it with a handkerchief. He began to hear birds singing. He didn't feel happy, but he felt all right, and at least he wasn't crying any more. He was in control of himself.

He went up to the road and started walking back toward Ilfeld, making a plan for the rest of the day as he went. Unpack trunk, get copy of railroad timetable, check schedule of church services, read *Grimm's Grammar* on the Latin past pluperfect. It was not a time to be unhappy. Easter was just over. Spring was just beginning, the first spring of a new century.

Get organized and begin to get things done. That was the answer.

Back in his room he found a package from Klaus on his bed. It was oblong and thickly padded, and inside was a small picture of Queen Louise in a narrow gold frame with a glass over it. More than a year before, he had given Klaus a picture of Ferdinand Lassalle, the German political philosopher who was Klaus's hero, to take with him to engineering school in Berlin, and now Klaus was returning the kindness. He turned the picture over. There was a note pinned to the back.

Otto!
Welcome to Ilfeld. Here is her Royal Highness, Auguste Wilhelmine Amalie Louise, to keep you company. As she overcame Napoleon, so must you overcome all of

those who dare to be your enemies. There's no German like a Scotch German!

Klaus

Otto imagined Klaus standing in some picture store in Berlin with a whole line of pictures in front of him, deciding which would be the right one to send, and then going back to his room and packing it with the skill of an engineer.

A good brother.

Otto put the picture on his desk and picked up his grammar. Work would make him feel better.

A week later he wrote his first letter to Ida.

Dear Ida,

Greetings from Ilfeld! This is my first official letter to you, and it comes with a hug and a tickle. You must keep it, so that when we are old we can read it together. Quickly put your nose in the envelope and you will smell a little bit of the wind that blows to us across the cold top of Brocken Mountain where the witches gather every year for a meeting. The witch stories, of course, are nonsense, but when I get home I will tell you a real old one that the farmers around here tell their children.

Louis and I are in excellent health, and we hope everybody at home is, too. He joins me in telling you to wear your watertight shoes on rainy days, keep warm, and do exactly what Mother tells you to do.

Guess what? We have a ghostly mystery at our school. Somebody here is a door thief! Last night our door was taken, and this afternoon it was found under the hay in the stable. Around here the door thief has a name. He's called "the carpenter's assistant." Isn't that a fine name?

Be good and happy. In thirty-one days I will write you again.

Love and kisses,

Otto

P.S. One of the horses in our stable is a great-grand-son of the horse General von Moltke rode in the war of 1870. I have not yet ridden him, but they say he is a fine animal.

In July he went back to Scotland for summer vacation. His father and mother had rented a house in Connel Ferry and everybody, including Klaus, was there. They sailed, they swam, they walked, and in the evening they did plays on the lawn by lanternlight. At the end of the month, as he stood at the rail of the ship going out of Glasgow harbor and watched his mother and sister waving goodbye, he cried again, but back in Ilfeld he plunged full speed into work, and by the end of November his room at the end of the stone walk had become home to him. Ilfeld, he decided, was exactly the kind of place he needed: it was demanding, it was busy, it was German, and the food was almost always good.

He had always known—his mother and father had taught him—that he was a special person, and that his family was a special family. The Kieps weren't like most of the Germans in Glasgow, and they weren't like any of the Scotch. Most of the people he knew, Scottish and German both, were respectable, trustworthy, intelligent, and fair—his teachers at Hillhead, for example, and the servants at home, and most of the men his father did business with. But none of them felt the same kind of high calling that he and his family felt. At Ilfeld he met students and teachers who felt a *German vocation* as strongly as he did. Coming there was like discovering his own tribe. "The Cloisterschool is my German birthplace," he wrote in a letter to his parents at the end of November. "I shall always be thankful to you for sending me here."

He was studying more, and exercising harder, than he ever had in his life. By Christmas he had grown an inch and a half over his summer height and gotten a little broader in the shoulders, though he was still very thin. (Every morning he lifted his desk chair, which was made of oak, fifty times over his head, and ran ten times around the outside of the school.)

In February he was named Primus of the Obertertia class. He began to find out what it felt like to be a person whose opinions about things carried weight. When, for example, the senior professor of Greek retired and the singing society wanted to have a concert beneath his window, they asked Otto what songs they should sing, even though he didn't know anything about music. And Otto, feeling an obligation to help them as best he could, spent an afternoon in the music room putting together a list of "farewell songs suitable for male voices."

Certainly there were a few people who didn't like him, but they were mostly stupid people, and he didn't like them, either. They made him feel helpless, and he did everything he could to stay out of their way.

That winter Otto took a course in German history under Max Wagner. Wagner's lectures were full of facts and dates and names, but never dry or cold, and always clear. He had visited all the important churches in Germany and Austria, and knew why each one was built, in what style, and how the plans were changed as the bishops got more or less money to spend. He knew the sources of family names, and the wanderings and wars of hundreds of Germanic clans. He could draw a detailed map of any part of Germany. When he spoke of "the superior Teutonic peoples" whose job it was to "complete the civilization of the world," he sounded scientific and passionate at the same time. And everyone in his classes knew whom he meant. He meant the boys at the desks in front of him, the German boys with good souls, good minds, good bodies, and rich fathers.

Otto could imagine him sitting in a garden talking to old Bismarck, and Bismarck listening for hours.

Wagner's ideas came chiefly from two men, Ernst Haeckel, who had just published a book called *The World Puzzle,* and Houston Stewart Chamberlain, whose book, *The Foundations of the Nineteenth Century,* had come out in 1898. Both Haeckel and Chamberlain were sure that Germanic people were by nature better than anybody else. Germany's great moment in history had arrived, they said, and the victory of German moral force was already beginning. "If we look around today," Chamberlain said, "we can see that the importance of each nation as a living power is only as great as the amount of truly Teutonic blood among its population."

Chamberlain's book was full of facts and beliefs and feelings and opinions and myths. Every sentence was bold and strong. Listening to Wagner reading Chamberlain out loud was like riding in a wagon pulled by fast horses across dangerous country. According to Chamberlain, the German man was better than anybody else in the world.

The Jews were the enemies of Teutonic purity, greedy and clever and corrupt. It was in their nature to hate goodness and culture. The German man had to stand against Jewish corruption and bring in a new age of morality, prosperity, and beauty.

Chamberlain and Haeckel were not special in their hatred of Jews. Many "Christian Europeans" felt the same way. Chamberlain himself was an Englishman, though he lived in Germany and wrote in German, and many Englishmen despised Jews as much as he did. In France there was a nation-wide Anti-Semitic League, and Russian and Polish Jews had been treated like dogs for centuries. What made Chamberlain and Haeckel special was their belief that just as Jews were *less* than human, "true Germans" were *more* than human. To their way of thinking, the Jews were at best *incomplete* people, unfinished and therefore not quite human. That's the way Professor Wagner saw it, and who could question such a careful, passionate, serious, and gentle man?

While considering the nature of the German man, Otto was asked to play the part of a German woman, the beautiful heroine in Lessing's play *Minna von Barnhelm*. He was a member of the Drama Club, and he had helped choose the play, so when Thomas Fluchtmann, the president, asked him to do it, he felt he had to say yes. He was too tall for the part, really, but his face was right, and his voice was sweet and not too low.

Minna von Barnhelm is a young woman of nineteen or twenty, good, beautiful, and intelligent, who is engaged to marry an army officer, Major von Tellheim. When the play opens, he has come upon hard times: his left arm has been hurt in battle, he has been put on half pay, and his rank has been taken away from him. Poor and disgraced, he feels that he must give up the woman he loves. Minna, helped by her maid Francesca, tries to persuade him that he is still an honorable man, and that love is stronger than anything else in the world. Finally, when he has tried to set her free for the last time, a letter arrives from the king calling him back to the army, restoring his rank, and assuring him of his fortune. Minna and he are free to live happily ever after.

Minna is really two persons at the same time. She is a young girl in love, longing to take her bridal vows and begin a new life, and she is a strong woman who wants her lover to treat her as an equal. She has the best part in the play, and Otto liked that.

January 26, 1901

Dear Ida—

I have a role in a play by the great German dramatist and philosopher Lessing! Ask Mother, and she will tell you all about him. It's great fun!

Every afternoon Thomas Fluchtmann and I go for a walk and recite our lines to each other, and now we have them perfect. I am playing a beautiful woman, and Thomas is playing a handsome, honorable officer. We love each other, but we both suffer a lot, and I play tricks on him, before we fall into each other's arms at the end. Won't I look funny dressed up in a long dress with a wig? I wish you were here to play the part for me. I'd stand up and clap louder than anyone else in the theater, and shout BRAVO and ENCORE until the roof shook, and you would have to take bow after bow in front of the curtain. And maybe some secret admirer would send you a dozen roses to be delivered on the stage at the end. You would be *wonderful.*

Ida wrote back right away asking him to draw a picture of himself in his costume and send it to her. He didn't. He did send a sketch, as a joke on himself, to Karl Wichmann, who was then teaching in England, but he asked him please never to show it to anyone.

One evening at dinner a boy at the next table said, in a loud voice, "I saw a girl in town today who walked just like Otto Kiep, except she wasn't as pretty." Everyone laughed. Otto smiled. A few days later he came back to his room and found a fan made of pigeon feathers on his bed. A week before the performance his picture of Queen Louise was missing, and that evening he found it over the entrance to the dining hall with a sign under it, QUEEN OTTO I. That made him mad. A German queen had been insulted and private property had been taken. He got a chair, and as he climbed up to get the picture down he said in a loud voice, "If the person who stole this picture from my room would like an honorable fight, I'll meet him in front of the stables at five tomorrow morning."

After he was in bed that night, Louis told him that he knew who had done it. "Don't tell me," Otto said. He didn't want to find out from somebody else, not even his brother. It was a matter of private honor, and if the thief didn't want to accept his challenge and reveal himself, then Otto didn't want to be bothered listening to his name. Besides, he had a good idea who it was—Hans

Werfel, an Unterprimaner. "I don't want to know," he said.

Louis shrugged. "He'll never come and fight you. There's no use getting up early tomorrow."

"Don't you get up," Otto said. "I'm just keeping a promise. Nothing will happen."

The next morning Otto got up at four-fifteen and washed himself all over with cold water. Louis got up too. They didn't say anything to each other, because they didn't have anything important to say. When they were dressed they had a drink from the bottle of brandy they kept on the bookshelf for special occasions, left the room, went along the stone corridor and out through the big oak door into the courtyard. It was snowing lightly. The air was very still and very cold.

The clock in the tower, standing gray against the gray sky, said four minutes to five. They started to walk toward the stables. Suddenly Otto was completely wide awake. He was sure Hans Werfel wouldn't be there, but that didn't matter. He was on his way to a duel, with nothing but brandy in his stomach. He was testing himself, making himself tougher, more of a man, more ready for the struggle in the world of men. They reached the stable.

There were five other boys there, and he and Louis came up to them and stood with them in a rough circle. It was possible that one of these boys was the picture thief, and might come flying at him when the clock struck five, so he tried to be ready and at the same time look relaxed. Behind him someone else started coming across the yard from the main building. Otto couldn't hear him—the snow made everything silent—but the other boys in the circle turned their heads and looked that way. The new person came up to the group and stood next to him. It was Thomas Siemens, who played the maid Francesca. Apparently he felt the girls had to stick together.

A minute went by and there was the little grinding sound that the clock always made before it struck, and then the bell in the tower banged five times.

"If the one who took the picture of Queen Louise is here, I'm ready to fight," Otto said.

Nobody answered or moved, and after a couple of minutes the boys in the circle began one by one to leave, shaking his hand before they went. Pretty soon only Louis and Thomas were left, and Otto knew that Thomas was not going to go. He wasn't the kind of boy who went without being told. He was lively, and not stupid, and Otto liked him, but there was something strange and unhealthy about him. He hung on to you. He couldn't stand being alone, and he wanted more than ordinary friendship. He wanted a friendship that was grown-up, serious, and permanent. He was like a worried girl looking for a husband.

He had chosen Otto to hang on to because Otto respected him and took him seriously. So, with the snow falling and the air cold and his stomach rumbling for food, Otto had to get rid of him without hurting his feelings. "We'd better go back to our rooms before we freeze," he said.

"Would you like a little something to warm you up?" Thomas asked. "You and Louis both. I have some of the best in my room."

Otto shook his head. "I have to do some reading and

keep my head clear," he said. "I'll see you this afternoon at rehearsal. Thanks for coming down for this."

The play was given on the weekend before Lent, with one Friday performance and two Saturday performances. It was a great success. Even Thomas Fluchtmann's Tellheim wasn't so bad, and Otto's Minna and Siemens's Francesca were great. Before the Friday performance Otto had stopped thinking of Minna as a woman. She was just a person he liked and wanted to show off, someone who did everything with her whole heart. Even in the final rehearsal, when he had to walk around on stage in the dress Mrs. Wagner had made for him, he stayed cool and said his lines the way he felt they ought to be said.

And then, when the Saturday night performance was over, he promised himself that he would never play a woman again as long as he lived.

The next morning, as usual, he went to church. Everybody always went. It was a rule. Nobody took attendance, but you were honor-bound to go. All the students were Protestants and going to church was part of everybody's confirmation vow. It was the clear public duty of all civilized Christian men.

Otto liked going to church because it brought him close to home, to his mother and father, and to Max and Ida and Louis and Klaus. It put him in touch with his past and, somehow, with his future, too. His pleasure in church was not religious in the usual sense of the word. His Protestant faith, in fact, was meaning less and less to him. He still loved the Easter hymns celebrating Christ's victory over death, and he still felt sadness on Good Friday as he thought of the Lord Jesus suffering on the cross, and he still thought that the Christmas story was the best story in the world, but he had changed. He wasn't a believer in the way he had been on the day he was confirmed.

Now he believed more in progress, and in the power of good men to know what was right and do it. He could see that back in the days of Jesus, when Jerusalem was full of ignorant Jews and cruel Romans, it made sense to talk about sin and look for the end of the world. But that was in the past, and things had changed. To Otto, St. Peter and St. Paul and John the Baptist were good but ignorant men. Certainly there was a lot of weakness and foolishness and injustice in the world—just think of the Glasgow slums—but the good people of the world, and especially the Germans, could overcome those "sins" without too much help from God. The only prayers he could pray seriously now were the Lord's Prayer and the prayer for German sailors.

So on the last Sunday before Lent, as Otto sat listening to a sermon about the sorrows of Christ, his mind was not on God, or on the world, but on home. He was remembering Sunday breakfast, the smell of toast, the taste of English jams, kippers, bacon and eggs, and strong coffee with hot milk and sugar in it.

IV

Back Home

THE five years at Ilfeld went by very fast, but when the last day came, in May 1905, it wasn't too sudden or too soon. Otto, who was now Cloister Primus, Primus Omnium, gave the graduation speech. The subject was "Family, Nation, and School." A good family, a noble country, and an excellent school, he said, are the world's greatest blessings, and the man who has known all three is honor-bound to spend his life seeking the truth, acting as a faithful friend, and serving his country.

For Otto, the best thing about the speech was that it gave his mother and father something to remember— their son Otto praising them in public. It was easy to do because he believed what he said. Without a strong family life, there could be no strong national life, and no private freedom or dignity, either. It was a short speech, very clear and very good.

After the ceremonies were over, his parents went to their hotel and Otto went back to his room to open the "honor letters" he had gotten from Ida and his brothers. Max, who was visiting a friend in Hanover, wrote a short letter saying that he hoped to follow Otto's good example. Louis, at the Naval Institute in Hamburg, wrote four pages recalling their years together as "brothers and brother scholars." Ida painted a big circle of ivy, heather, and roses with the words "Congratulations to My Brother Otto on the Occasion of His Graduation" inside. Klaus's letter from Berlin was written in gold ink on dark brown paper. It was four words long: "Ha' a bonnie day."

Otto put the letters in his pocket and walked to the hotel to pick up his parents. From there they went to the Tanne Inn, where his fraternity was having a dinner party. The Zechonia brothers were faithful to the Tanne. It was the only place they would buy their beer. (Brandy was another matter. You brought that from home.) Sitting at the "high table" eating good food, he felt wonderful. His two families were together—the family he belonged to, and the family that belonged to him. Five years before, there had been only four Zechonia brothers, including himself and Louis. Now there were eighteen, most of whom had come in because of his persuasion, a happy family of men getting ready to build a better Germany and a better world.

The only thing that was wrong was his mother's dress. It was made of a stiff, dark, shiny cloth, like the upholstery on the seats of second-class railroad cars. The way the sleeves drooped made her shoulders look fat and round, and the whole thing hung on her like a curtain.

His father was different. Moving his neat little white beard up and down as he chewed his food, he was a model of elegance. Johannes Kiep knew how to dress for the world, and Otto admired that.

Oh well, his mother had spirit, and that was more important.

Monday morning, after his trunk had been sent off for home and the last goodbyes had been said, he and his parents got on the train to Berlin. Klaus met them at the station and they went to the home of Max Kosmack, a cousin and good friend of his mother's, who had a large house in Berlin-Steglitz. The next evening he took them to the Metropole Theater to see a musical comedy revue. It was the first time Otto had ever seen one, and he loved it. From then on, it was his favorite kind of show.

They stayed at the Kosmacks' until Thursday. Every morning Otto and his father went for a walk and talked. Mr. Kiep told him about the business and how it was changing. Most of his timber was now coming from Russia, and that made him uneasy. The Russian merchants delivered on time, and he always got exactly what he ordered, but he didn't like having to depend so much on one country. Russia was close to revolution. A thousand protestors had been shot to death on the steps of the Winter Palace in January, and now there was talk of a national strike. Still, they went on selling at the best prices, so he had no choice.

They talked about where Otto should study law. He wanted to get both a British and a German degree, and his father was enthusiastic about that. They talked about what army regiment he should join for his year of military training after his studies were over. And again and again, they talked about the business. He reminded Otto that it was an important part of the Kiep family history. Their entire fortune had been built upon it. The firm was part of the German outreach to the world. A German family doing well in Glasgow was more important than a German family doing well in Berlin or Hamburg. And Otto had the talents for the job—except for his handwriting, which his father noticed had become terrible in the last few years.

Still, in spite of all these good and forceful reasons, he told Otto that he was free to decide for himself whether to enter the business or stay out of it. In the next months he would get a chance to know the business better. Then he could study law, and do his military service, and when those things were done, make a decision.

On Monday morning, May 8, 1905, Otto began work in the firm of Carl Kiep and Brother, Timber Merchants.

When Otto was a boy, the firm had occupied a double office at 116 St. Vincent's Street. There were seventeen other businesses in the same building, including a picture-frame maker, a wine merchant, a mercantile insurance company, and three accountants. Only one tenant, Mr. John Barr, an assessor of fire losses, had a telephone. Everyone else depended completely upon messenger boys and the mail. It was a crowded, busy building, with two or three people always on the stairway.

In 1898, just before Johannes Kiep was made Consul, he moved the firm to the second floor of the building at

128 St. Vincent's Street. It was a quieter, more dignified place. The top floor was occupied by a firm of solicitors— Holms, Mactavish, and M'Killop—and the first floor by the National Bank of Scotland. It was the kind of building in which an Imperial Consul could feel at home, and "extend himself" a little.

Otto's workday began at seven-thirty and ended at five-thirty, with an hour off for lunch. He had two jobs. One was to keep track of the day-to-day cash transactions of the firm—money put out for such things as postage, package charges, trolley fares for messengers, tea for the office teapots, odd stationery, and so on. At the end of the week he wrote a "summary accounting" and submitted it to Mr. Anderson, who was in charge of the small-cash drawer.

His other job, which took him completely by surprise, was taking dictation. The morning of his second day at work his father called him in and began dictating a letter. He talked so fast Otto couldn't keep up. All he could do was take notes on the important parts and make sure that he got all the numbers down. When his father was finished, Otto went back to the outer office, went over to Anderson's desk, and told him what had happened.

"What language was it in?" Anderson asked.

"German."

Anderson went and brought over Herr Böhm, the German correspondence clerk. Böhm was very calm and philosophical. "Your father won't notice anything as long as we have the sense right. I know his style. Just show me your notes. Are you sure you have the figures right?"

He put the letter together, and Otto typed it out on

the German typewriter and brought it in to his father before lunch. Böhm had been perfectly right. He didn't notice a thing, but merely signed it and told Otto to put it with the rest of the outgoing mail.

That afternoon Otto borrowed Herr Böhm's copy of the Stolze-Schrey German shorthand book, and started spending his lunch hours and most of his evenings studying and practicing. After three weeks he could keep up with his father no matter how fast he dictated. Then he began to work on English shorthand, but at a slower pace.

He was ashamed of being afraid of his father. Grownup sons, unless they were cowards, were supposed to respect their fathers without fear. He couldn't. Johannes Kiep was an honest, fair-minded, good man, but whenever he was near him, he felt like a little boy.

In everything the Consul did, now, there was a kind of angry seriousness that he had never seen before. Johannes Kiep was busy trying to get as much pleasure as he could out of his position before he had to give it up. When she married him, Mrs. Kiep made him promise that he would retire to Germany when he became sixty. He was now fifty-eight. Germany was his home—it was the place he wanted to go to die when the time came—but in Germany he would be just another rich old man on a pension, and he hated that.

But there was nothing he could do. He had no choice. He had promised. Already Mrs. Kiep was getting weekly reports from Klaus about furnished apartments in Berlin. And she wasn't going to wait two years to move. She was going to go in October, and her husband could follow her when he was ready.

No wonder he had such a serious, almost fierce way with his workers.

As soon as he had learned his duties, and the newness of office work had worn off, Otto started to get restless. He was enjoying the company of Ida and his mother—and enjoying being enjoyed by them—and he was doing a lot of sailing and swimming, and he was earning fifty shillings a week for the first time in his life, but still he was restless. His life was suspended between childhood and manhood, between getting ready for the university and going there, between the power he had known as Cloister Primus and the power he would some day know as Doctor of Law.

The only person who saw his situation clearly was Dr. Wichmann, who came up from Lincoln for a visit at the end of August. He and Otto spent a day together sailing near Hunter's Quay in a lugsail boat borrowed from the yacht club. It was a beautiful day, with a strong southwest breeze. The skies were clear, the sun was warm, and they had a basket full of food that Francis, the cook, had packed for them. Otto did the sailing, and Wichmann sat down low in the center of the boat smoking his pipe and watching the water.

After lunch he told Otto how it had been, working as a tutor in the Kiep house. "It was not entirely free from difficulties," he said, though he had "never had any serious reason to complain." The Consul was not to be blamed for being an *energetic* man. Energy was part of his fine character. It was part of Mrs. Kiep's character, too, but in a different way.

He asked Otto how he felt about the firm. Would he join it when he got through at the university? Otto shook his head. No, he was sure he wouldn't. He was learning some important things—the shorthand would help at the university, and it was useful to see modern business from the point of view of the minor clerk—but on the other hand, he didn't know much more now than he had known seven years before when he was showing Dr. Wichmann around the timber wharf. It was good being in Glasgow again, but Germany was home, and he would be glad to get back there.

As they started to tack toward the harbor, Wichmann spoke about Ida. She was in some ways like the Consul, he said. Her eyes were like his, and she had the same serious attitude toward the world. But her seriousness was different. It was deeper, a kind of *melancholy*. She needed to be drawn out of herself, he said, to "strengthen the happy part of her nature through exercise." Children of her age often made solemn and private religious vows at their confirmation. He had done it himself, vowing to pray and read the Bible every day of his life, no matter how sick or busy he was. He had kept the vow a long time, too. Had she perhaps made some such vow at her confirmation?

Otto didn't know, but one thing was clear—Ida did not want to leave Scotland. She had grown up there, she was more at ease speaking English than speaking German, and there was a girl living at the end of Hughenden Terrace, Gladys McDonald, whom she loved. Maybe, too, she was afraid of German schools. In English schools, a child was expected to be good, to be a lady or a gentleman. In German schools even girls were expected to be smart, and Ida did not think she was smart, no matter what Otto said.

The worst thing, from Otto's point of view, was that she seemed to see Berlin as a kind of punishment, something she had to go through for the purification of her soul. "In her spirit, she's the oldest one of us," he said.

V

Trude

I N the fall of 1905 the Kiep family—except for the Consul—moved from Glasgow to Berlin. Mrs. Kiep rented a six-room apartment on the Nürnberger Platz in which Otto, Klaus, Ida, Mrs. Kiep, a maid from the Glasgow home named Jane, and "Aunt Lollo," the unmarried sister of a friend of Mrs. Kiep's, lived together. The absolute head of the house was Mrs. Kiep, who woke everyone up at six-thirty every day no matter how late they had gone to bed the night before, and always had a job for anyone who didn't know what to do.

Within a month, Ida had found a friend, a lovely girl named Illi Grisson. They played together every afternoon, and met Otto two or three times a week as he got off the trolley from the university. One of the things that held them together was their belief that Otto was the best man in the world. Sometimes, on Saturday afternoon, he would take them to a chocolate shop and say, "Buy whatever you want." He was really a kind of a god.

From the beginning, Otto felt completely at home in Berlin because of Klaus, who was already a Berliner.

Klaus knew where every trolley went, and which restaurants were cheap but had good food, and when everything opened and closed. He knew waiters, ticket sellers, tailors, students, museum guards, musicians, and dozens of girls, some of whom he treated like sisters and some of whom he treated like wives. He belonged to a circle of families, all with young unmarried sons and daughters, who gave wonderful balls and parties—the Schmidtleins, the Körtes, the Wendelstadts, the Köhns, the von Mendelsohns, and a few others. They were all good, close families, most of them with at least three children. They weren't among the richest families in Berlin, but all of them had enough money to do the things they thought were important—going to concerts and the theater, having really good music teachers for their children, bringing in a tutor once a week to keep the family up on its French or English, and traveling to interesting places— Egypt, Greece, France, the North Sea.

There were a number of "social circles" in Berlin, and parties and balls went on all the time. If a young man could talk and listen and dance, he got more invitations than he could handle. But the Köhn circle was different. It put a higher value on conversation, and nothing was "too delicate" to talk about, not politics or music or money or love or anything else.

Early in January 1907, Klaus and Otto went to a post-Christmas party at the Wendelstadts. Twelve or fifteen small tables had been put at one end of the big double living room of their apartment, and at the other end, across a wide, polished floor, stood a grand piano. Otto found his name card at a table for four. Two other people were already there, fighting. One was a girl of about eighteen in a pink and ivory gown, and the other was a young army lieutenant in his dress uniform. The girl was Trude Köhn. Otto introduced himself, and the officer stood up and shook hands and then sat down again to resume his argument.

He began to explain to Miss Köhn, in a somewhat loud voice, why soldiers were better than students. He used himself as an example. What was he doing? He was turning young, uneducated, raw recruits into useful citizens, people their country could be proud of. What a far different life that was from the one students led. "These so-called students," he said, "what are they doing when we, at six o'clock in the morning, are already out with our men? They drink and sleep the whole night. What do they care? And what do they do for our people? They steal God's good day."

Miss Köhn looked at him as if he was a child. "But isn't what you do very dull?"

"What is dull and what is not dull, Miss Köhn, doesn't come into question. We are building men."

"But you must have some free time. What books have you read recently?"

The lieutenant shook his head. "You don't begin to understand. You are asking a typical student question. My work is of a completely different kind."

"Well, I'm sure you read *military* books," she said, "histories of battles and weapons and great generals. Do you go to concerts? Perhaps you have a chance to take some of your men to such things."

"You haven't the slightest understanding of military life."

"Music can be very patriotic sometimes, don't you think?"

"Music is a very small part of the military life, Miss Köhn," he said, and then began again explaining his work. While he talked, a light supper was served, and during coffee Otto took Miss Köhn's dance card and wrote his name next to the first and third quadrilles and the last waltz. Then he put it back in front of her plate and nodded to her. A minute or so later, the music began.

During the next three hours there was hardly a break in the music as two pianists, one a professional and the other a friend of the family, took turns playing. Otto danced with ten or twelve young women, but he always kept his eye on Trude so that he'd be close enough to take her hand for the first notes of his three dances.

He had never come upon anybody like her before, even in his imagination. There was something absolutely fresh about her, as if she had just come out of the woods after a long, silent, and interesting walk. She was simple and direct and beautiful. Dancing with her was like being carried away by an angel. He decided that he would marry her.

During the next few months he danced with her at ten or fifteen parties and balls. He met her mother and father, and her younger sister Line, who was sixteen, and her four younger brothers. He became a "member of the circle," and when he couldn't make it to a party at the Wendelstadts' or the Körtes' or the Grisebachs', people asked Klaus where he was, and when Klaus wasn't there either, they asked Trude.

The Köhns owned a modest villa in Grunewald with

large, good rooms. There were never enough chairs for everyone, but there were always a lot of cushions around, and the young men in their formal suits and the girls in their gowns would sit on the floor to eat or sing or listen to music, and get up and go to the other end of the room, where the piano was, to dance. The great test for a newcomer was whether, seeing everyone sitting on the floor, he would sit down and join the crowd or stand stiffly near the wall.

A ball at the Köhns' began with Rudolph Klutmann singing, accompanied by Victor Wendelstadt, serious and happy songs by Schubert, Brahms, Schumann, and Wolf, and always ended with everyone singing folk and student songs. In between there was dancing, and good food, and the look and smell of fresh flowers.

Trude's grandparents owned a house on Lake Wannsee, a trolley-car ride from Berlin. Across the lake was an estate, "The Cladow," which belonged to friends of theirs. There, during the summer of 1907, the circle of families went on good Saturdays. The estate had once been farmed, but all the land was now either lawn or meadow or forest. Near the water was a small caretaker's cottage in which an old couple lived, the chimney sticking out through the bushes. Beyond a wide lawn with huge old trees there was an old yellow house with a large living room and, in the hall, an out-of-tune piano. Most of the circle went across the lake by boat, though a few parents went around by road and some younger brothers talked of *running* around and beating everybody there. The Kieps had bought a second-hand sailboat, and Otto and Klaus would load it with people and picnic baskets and sail it across, giving the rowboaters a ten-minute head start.

When everyone had landed, the girls would set tables and unpack the food while the men made fires and played with the younger children. After lunch they often played a Scottish game of tag, "Warning, Warning, Three Times Warning," which Otto and Klaus had taught them, and softball, and went for long walks, and swam.

Before sundown they ate again, and watched the sunset, and then someone would sit down at the piano and begin to play, and inside and outside the house the men and women danced while younger brothers and sisters played tag, or watched, or went down to the shore and skipped stones across the surface of the moonlit lake.

Around eleven, with lanterns on the boats, they left Cladow and started home. Usually, Otto and Klaus could sail their boat before the wind straight across the lake. Hans Klutmann always came along, and he would stand next to the mast, with a lantern at his feet, and sing one song after another into the dark, always ending with his favorite, "The Three Grenadiers." Sometimes, when the boats were all tied up and everyone was ashore, they would decide not to take the streetcar but to walk home instead through the cool woods.

On the afternoon of the last Saturday in October, Otto sailed with Trude and Line across the lake and up the river Havel, where they left the boat in a dockyard for the winter. They hurried back along the river and around the lake, carrying the sails and gear between them. The Klingler String Quartet was playing that night at the Academy, and Line had promised Mr.

Klingler she'd be there. When they arrived they could hear the musicians tuning up inside. They left the sails and gear next to the wall near the entrance, and got to their seats with about ten seconds to spare.

Otto was now beginning his third year of law studies, the "serious year," and he decided to become engaged to Trude after his first law examinations were over in the summer of 1908. His mother and Ida and Illi Grisson were in Glasgow, where the Consul was going through a series of farewell parties and visits, and this gave him more time to himself. He went back over all his shorthand lecture notes for the past two years, transcribing them on the typewriter, and began to drill for his exams under a well-known "Repetitor," Mr. Gerhardt.

During the fall and winter he saw Trude once a week or so, at parties and musicals, but he never mentioned his plans to her. Why should he? She was his ideal woman, honest and beautiful and pure, and he didn't want to do anything to change her in any way. Within a year she would be a fiancée, and soon after that a wife, and then a mother. Let her, for a little while longer, be a perfect virgin with no special plans.

In March 1908, the Great Köhn Party took place on all four floors of their house in the Grunewald. The top floor was the Mountain House, where there were games for the younger children and pretzels, cheese, toast, and a barrel full of "wine for travelers." From the Mountain House, guests went down to the next floor, the Village, on a slide made out of smooth, soaped boards laid on the stairs. In the Village was a traveling circus. Line did a trapeze act, there were various wild animals, and finally there was a bullfight. Walter Gropius, a young architecture student, and one of the Grisebach boys were the bullfighters, dressed up in real Spanish bullfight costumes.

At four-thirty a "play of high tragedy" took place on the second floor. A mountain had been built out of tables and mattresses. In front of it was a tub full of water, and next to the tub was a park bench with a sign, "Wet paint." A boy came along and took the sign away. A pair of lovers—Klaus dressed as an army officer and Otto wearing a long skirt and a curly yellow wig—came and sat down and declared their love for one another in long, passionate speeches. When they got up they both had white stripes on them. The angry soldier ran around until he found the boy behind a bush and called the police. An enormously fat policeman arrived and started chasing the boy around and around and up and down the hill. Then the boy fell into the lake, and as he jumped out the policeman slid in. By now the tub was almost empty, the floor was covered with water, the audience was screaming and jumping around, parents and nursemaids were beginning to arrive to pick the children up, and a few older people were already arriving to dance in the "Inn in the Valley," which was on the first floor.

And Mr. Köhn was beginning to look a little upset.

Otto and Trude and Klaus got mops and rags from the cleaning closet and started mopping up and carrying buckets full of water to the sinks in the washing room at the back of the house. They carried the empty tub out and took the wet mattresses up to the Mountain House to dry. They worked for almost two hours, and when they were done, Otto and Trude went upstairs to say good night to her brothers, who were by then in bed, and to talk, in whispers, about how wonderful everything had been. Then they went downstairs and danced.

Two nights a week beginning in November he and his friend Oskar Weigert taught reading and writing to a group of Berlin workers at the Workers' School. After class they usually went with their students to a *Bierstube,* where they drank beer and talked. Around midnight he would take a trolley home.

Oskar was a Jew. He never talked about being a Jew, and if you had asked him what he was, he would have said he was a German, or a European, or a Socialist. But one night, over beer and rolls, after their students had all gone home, they began discussing the history of France, and Oskar talked about the "idea of Jewishness" and how it had been used by French bankers and bishops and priests and schoolteachers and kings and storekeepers as an excuse for war and robbery and revolution and murder. "And, as you know, the long swindle is not over," he said. "Half the men in our class would be glad to see every Jew in Germany put in a barrel and shipped to America, as long as they leave their money behind."

"So," Otto said, "we need more education."

Oskar shook his head. "The professors are no better. As a Jew, I would trust our students more than I would trust the philosophy professors at the university. They would find a hundred clever reasons to nail our barrels shut. There are people I work with, people who treat me with kindness and even respect, who feel in their hearts that

Jews are a disease to be cured. A Jew has few friends in Europe, even among other Jews."

"You can count me one, I think," Otto said.

Oskar nodded. "I do."

In June he passed his Referendar examination, which was much easier than he had expected. The Köhns were already at their summer house in Ahrenshoop on the East Sea. He decided to go there and begin his official courtship in mid-July. Then, in August, he would go to London for his Bachelor of Laws examination.

His parents were living in Ballenstedt, in the Harz Mountains. The Consul had investigated and found that Ballenstedt was one of the places in Germany where men lived to be very old, and since he didn't believe in an afterlife, and hated the idea of death, he was going to get as many years as he could. Ida, of course, was living with them.

His brothers were spread all over Germany. Klaus had taken a job with a ship-repairing firm in Hamburg, Max was studying law in Kiel, and Louis was somewhere pursuing his naval career. Without his family, and without Trude, and with no more work to do, Otto found Berlin a very empty place. He left on Sunday, July 5, to spend his birthday with his parents in Ballenstedt before going on to see the Köhns.

In Ballenstedt he found carpenters and plumbers and plasterers all over the house. Mrs. Kiep had decided to add three bathrooms, enlarge the kitchen, make two rooms out of three on the second floor, and add a greenhouse like the one behind the Glasgow house, only bigger. The Ballenstedt natives had decided that the Kieps were planning to turn the house into a hotel, and that Mrs. Kiep, whom they called "the Englishwoman," was trying to imitate Queen Victoria. The Consul and Otto's mother had already established their daily routine when he arrived. Mrs. Kiep took tea, English fashion, every afternoon, sometimes with his father, sometimes with guests, and often alone. On the day before his birthday, as Otto and his mother were drinking tea in the garden, he told her of his plan to go to the Köhns' and "state his intentions" with regard to Trude.

His mother was delighted. Trude, she said, was an excellent young woman in every way. Otto went over to her chair and hugged and kissed her, and then he sat down again and they talked about Trude's virtues until the tea got cold and the sun was down behind the house. They agreed that the Consul should not know anything until after Otto had talked with the Köhns and "established a firm connection." The Consul would more likely be for the marriage if Trude's parents, whom he liked and admired, were won over first. And certainly they would be. Everyone in both families, she said, falling into English, would soon enough see that he and Trude were a "good match."

Otto left for Ahrenshoop two days later. Before he left he was alone with his father several times, and each time he wanted to tell him his plans, but he couldn't. He was afraid. He did tell him, however, that he was going to see the Köhns at their summer home, and his father seemed delighted.

He arrived in Ahrenshoop early in the morning of the eleventh and walked to the Köhn house along the beach. Mrs. Köhn was home alone—everyone else was out picking berries—and she gave him two telegrams. He went up to his room, which faced the front of the house, sat down in a chair near the window, and opened the first. It was from his father: "REFRAIN FROM ANY BINDING STEP UNTIL WE HAVE SPOKEN." His mother's telegram said: "I SUPPORT YOUR FATHER'S REASONABLE REQUEST."

His courtship was over. His father would tell him not to see Trude, and he would obey. That's all there was to it. There was no use hoping for other possibilities. It was done. *Everything* was over. His father would demand surrender, and get it.

He could see the path of his life laid out in front of him. He would never marry—that was as clear as the sunlight coming in through the window. He would always live alone. And Trude would marry some smooth, older man, and they would live a quiet, elegant life together, taking walks on Sunday afternoon, raising good-looking, polite children, and living to a happy old age. But her husband, no matter how long he knew her, would never be able to see what he saw in her, or understand how absolutely perfect she was.

He sat alone for a long time, until he heard Trude and Line come into the house. A minute or so later the Köhn boys ran in the front door, through the house, and out the back. He got up, put the telegrams in his suitcase, tried to put a happy, easy look on his face, and went downstairs. Trude was in the living room hooking up a window curtain that had come loose. The house was quiet. Everyone else seemed to have disappeared. She turned around when he came in, and in that moment he silently said goodbye to her.

"Otto. Everybody's been wondering when you were coming."

"I just got here about an hour ago. How's the water?"

"Perfect. We're all going swimming late this afternoon, and have dinner on the beach."

"Good."

They were silent for a few moments. "We'll go for a walk this afternoon," she said. "I'll show you where we found a whole treasure house of wild strawberries."

While they were walking to the strawberry field she asked him a dozen questions—how his parents were and what Klaus was doing and whether Ida had enjoyed her time in Glasgow and so on. He answered all her questions carefully, especially the ones about the house in Ballenstedt, which he knew she would never see. He suddenly felt completely abandoned. The one perfect and beautiful girl was walking beside him for almost the last time. Part of his life was ending. But she didn't know it. She walked on in her easy, open, natural way, her back straight, her eyes on the trees ahead.

The next morning when everyone else went over to the old inn for coffee and buns, he asked Mrs. Köhn if he could talk to her. They went out into the garden and sat down on a bench, and he told her what his situation was. He had the telegrams with him and showed them to her.

She read them carefully, thinking about what they said and what they did not say. She gave him the telegrams back and they sat in silence for a few moments, looking at each other. She was thirty-eight years old, and though she had six children and led a demanding life, she was still a very lovely woman, with clear skin and young eyes. (She swam and hiked a good deal, and Otto knew from experience that she was a better dancer than either of her daughters.) She smiled at him, and said that she had watched him with Trude for a long time and knew how he felt about her. In fact, she and Mr. Köhn had already talked about him as someone who might want to marry Trude, and had decided that the two of them should be allowed to make up their own minds. "Whatever decision you make, to go to her directly or withdraw, we will continue to respect you and your family."

They went on to talk, briefly, about his plans, and he told her of his expected appointment for a year's military service with the Oldenburg Dragoons. He began to praise Trude again, but Mrs. Köhn stopped him. If he wanted to say good things about Trude, he should say them to her and not to her parents. After a short while he stood up and shook hands with her, and while they were shaking hands he leaned over and kissed her on the cheek.

The rest of the weekend was a strange, silent, and sad dream. On Monday morning he said goodbye to Mrs. Köhn, and he and Trude walked together to the dock. Along the side of the road yellow Swedish clover was growing, and as they walked along in silence Trude picked a going-away bouquet for him. They said goodbye, shook hands, she gave him the flowers, and he got on the boat. After it pulled away from the dock he stood waving for a few minutes, but then he went inside the little cabin, while she continued to stand on the dock. His last sight of her was of a tall figure in a white dress waving her right arm slowly, almost lazily, back and forth.

When he got home he went to see his mother first. She was writing letters in her study. She told him that his father had come to her right after his departure and insisted that she tell him everything she knew about his plans. She *had* to tell him. She had no choice.

He assured her that he understood. It was *hiding* the truth that was wrong, not telling it. His father had only asked what he had a right to know. As he talked about his father's rights his mother's face became hard and hateful, so he stopped, kissed her, and crossed the house to his father's study.

His father didn't seem angry with him at all. He greeted him like an old and respected customer who had come in to talk over a business matter of mutual interest. He asked Otto to sit down. The Köhn family, he said, had his highest respect. A marriage between the two families would be a good and desirable thing. Klaus and Line, for example, would make a good pair in two or three years—she would be eighteen or nineteen and Klaus would be twenty-nine or thirty and well established in his work. As for Otto and Trude . . . well, that, unfortunately, was a different matter. Everything was against it. He had not done his court work in Leipzig, or his doctoral thesis, or his assessor's exam, or his English law exam, or his year of army training. And when all that was done, he would not even have *begun* his career. Clearly, it was impossible for him to ask any girl and her family to wait so long. Trude was a fine girl, and she had a right to marry an established man. It was unfortunate. He had once been young, and he understood such disappointments, but facts were facts and had to be faced.

He didn't realize how much he needed a friend, or how good a friend Oskar Weigert was, until he got back to Berlin. He had given Oskar a key to his apartment so that he could use his law books, and when he opened his door on the evening of his first day back in Berlin, Oskar was sitting at his desk, reading.

Oskar had the face of a man who had gone through all the major victories and defeats of human life at least once, and was ready to go through them all again. There was a bottle of wine and some rolls and cheese mixed in with the books on the desk, and while they ate and drank Otto told him what had happened. Oskar listened, asked a few short questions, and then sat still for a minute or so, looking at the stem of his wine glass.

"It is absolutely finished?"

"Yes."

"It's a great loss. A person like Trude Köhn is rare."

"I'll never meet anyone like her."

They were silent again, and then Oskar began talking about his doctoral dissertation. For the first time since he got the two telegrams Otto began to feel like a person again. He could see ahead a little way, and imagine himself living in the world.

VI

Interlude

He took his first British law examinations at the Imperial Institute, London, at the end of August 1909, and on October 1 entered the Oldenburg Dragoon Regiment 192 for a year of military training. His time in the army was good. He met a lot of men he liked, he enjoyed the field exercises, the barrack parties, and even the parades. The following September he was discharged with the rank of reserve lieutenant. He went immediately to Nauen, where he worked at the local court (the Amtsgericht) for two months and then transferred to the district court (the Landgericht) in Neuruppin.

In the summer of 1911 he went to London to study and do some social work in the London slums with Barclay Baron, an English friend. He took the English Bachelor of Laws exam in September, and failed. He returned to Germany with two crates of books and took up his law apprenticeship again. The following summer he went back for the English exam and passed. In September 1912 he was home in Ballenstedt to celebrate his birthday, two months late. Louis and his wife weren't there for the celebration, but Klaus and Max came, and of course Ida, who was living at home. There was a big family party with a lot of good wine and an enormous *Baisertorte* with whipped cream. Klaus gave a speech about the joys of old age, and Ida recited a poem she had written in his honor.

Ida had a friend with her at the party, a man named Walter Westphal. He was the sort of good, gentle man Otto had always wanted Ida to meet and fall in love with. Now, in spite of himself, he felt jealous and a little bit angry. He and Ida had made an agreement in the summer of 1909 that neither of them would ever get married—that Ida would some day come and live with him, run his house, and serve as hostess for his parties. It had been her idea, and he had agreed to it only because he knew how important it was to her at the time. It was one of those promises which are made to be broken. Now, to his complete surprise, he resented her for breaking it.

After the party, and after Walter had gone home, the two of them walked out past the greenhouse together and she talked about what a wonderful man Walter was. They had an "understanding," she said, and wanted to marry as soon as possible, but she had not forgotten her "sisterly promise" to him, and would only marry if he released her from it. If he didn't, she was ready to give Walter up and come and live with him whenever he wanted her.

She was completely serious, and Otto knew it. He put his arm around her and kissed her on the cheek. Of course he would set her free from her promise. But she would have to wait a little while before he could really be happy about the idea of her marriage. It would happen soon enough, he said, and then he and Walter would be the best of friends.

After she went back into the house, Otto stayed in the garden. He was disappointed at himself. He was being selfish and cold. Well, he would *work* at being glad about Ida's marriage. He would *make* himself be glad. It was the only right thing to do.

He was not surprised to find that the Consul was against the marriage. Walter Westphal was not rich, and he was not ambitious. There was, then, no good reason to approve of him. At breakfast the next morning, with no warning, Mr. Kiep looked at Ida and said, "Ida, you were not born to marry a farmer." For a minute she didn't move, and then she got up slowly, trying to keep her dignity, left the table and went to her room. Otto poured milk into his coffee. "I think I'll go over to Wedderstedt this afternoon and see Mr. Westphal and look at his estate," he said.

He left right after lunch, and got to Wedderstedt about three. Walter was surprised to see him, and took him on a tour of the buildings and fields that were part of the estate. As they went along, Otto got a better idea of the kind of man Walter Westphal was. He was a country man—not interested in cities or in what happened in them. He seemed to feel that God would some day judge him for two things, how well he had used his land, and how fairly he had treated the men and women who got their living from it. He was one of those men who look as if they had been born wise and a little sad. He was an old-style German living in the new Germany, where the estate owner had to make way for the banker, the factory owner, and the engineer. The Westphals had lost money and power, but in Walter they still had their sense of responsibility and their dignity.

Otto left feeling that he had found a friend. His bitterness and jealousy were gone. He would do everything he could to help Ida marry this man.

He got a letter from his father in November saying that he wanted Ida to "go on a trip and forget her farmer." Mrs. Kiep was going with her, and he wanted Otto to go too. They would leave in late January and be gone nine weeks, visiting Milan, Lake Maggiore, Rome, Beaulieu-sur-Mer, and Monte Carlo. He would, naturally, take care of Otto's expenses.

Otto agreed, but said he would have to leave the trip after five weeks because he had to be in Leipzig to help prepare a case early in March.

They left on January 20, and for the next five weeks Ida and Otto lived under the absolute dictatorship of Mrs. Charlotte Kiep, Master Tour Leader and Menu Suggester. (Otto was allowed one decision a day. He could choose the dinner wine and order it.) Every morning she appeared for breakfast in one of her heavy, horrible-looking dresses, with a "program for the day" in her hand. Otto and Ida felt like little children on a Sunday outing at the zoo.

The aim was to keep Ida so busy that she had no time to think about Walter during the day, and was too tired to think about him or write letters to him at night. Of course she wrote him at least once a day, and every few days, no matter how tired she was, she would sneak out of her room and go for a midnight walk with Otto. His job on these walks was to listen to her worries, cheer her up, and protect her from saying things she would later be sorry for.

Their last night in Rome—Otto was going to leave for Leipzig in four or five days—she asked him to meet her in front of her room at midnight. Her door opened exactly on time, and the two of them went side by side, without talking, down the long, carpeted hall to the stairs. The hotel was completely silent, and even the cleaning man they passed brushing the stair carpet was working noiselessly.

A light rain was blowing as they started down the front steps of the hotel. It felt good. "You will find this hard to believe," Otto said as they turned right and started along the wide, empty sidewalk, "but I saw a large angel in the hall while I was waiting for you. He had a glass of beer in one hand and a roll in the other." Ida asked him what the angel's name was. "Sidney," Otto said. The angel's specialty was watching over lawyers and young women in love. This work kept him very busy, so he had to eat and drink on the job. He was now paying special attention to the case of Miss Ida Kiep, a young woman of most unusual abilities and deep feelings who was traveling through Italy in the company of her lovely mother and her talented and extraordinarily handsome older brother.

They stopped for a few moments in front of a store window where there was a display of silver jewelry. "You would never believe what he told me," Otto said.

"Yes, I would."

"Honor bright?"

"Honor bright, every word."

They started walking again, and Otto told his story. The angel, he said, had shown him a large portrait, in a gold frame, of a very intelligent-looking male pig. In a former life, the angel told him, this pig had been a knight in the court of King Arthur, fighting bravely against dragons, witches, and so forth. Now he was a knightly pig on a large estate in Wedderstedt, Germany, where at this very moment his heart was beating wildly with joy because a Lady was coming to whom he could dedicate his entire fat, beautiful, and intelligent self.

But, Otto had asked the angel, what good would it do for a Lady to be loved by a pig, even if the pig was once a knight?

The angel replied that it was far better to be loved by a knightly pig than by a piggy knight. And besides, this pig had the magic power of changing all of his Lady's enemies into very small and harmless spiders, and of bringing happiness to all her children. After that, Otto said, the angel and the portrait disappeared, but not before the angel had given him "a token of his protection." He stopped under a streetlight, took out a box, and gave it to her. Inside was a small silver pin with the figure of an angel on it. Ida pulled Otto down to her and kissed him. There were tears in her eyes.

On Easter 1914, Ida Kiep became Ida Westphal. The celebration was beautiful (and very expensive), and no one had a better time than Otto.

VII

The War Begins

On August 1, 1914, war began. Europe had been slowly and politely moving toward war for years, but when it came, people were taken completely by surprise. Berlin, that bright, happy, superior city, became gray and quiet in an hour. Rumors ran everywhere, that a French flier had dropped bombs on Nuremberg, that the Japanese had entered the war on the side of Germany, that a Russian spy had been caught at the Swinemünde railroad station carrying a bottle of germs to infect the water supply, and that a German sergeant with another bottle of germs had been arrested and shot in Danzig.

All of a sudden, everyone looked ten years older. The only ones who seemed to have any sweetness or youth left were the soldiers, who showed a special care for strangers and did double duty to help each other. They alone seemed to remember that it was summer, and that the flowers were blooming.

Otto had orders to join his regiment in Oldenburg. He left Berlin on the morning of August 2 and went to Ballenstedt. He had to see his father before he went into battle. For six years they had been enemies—polite, correct, cold, and distant. Otto gave him legal advice, went for walks with him during holidays home, and wrote a birthday letter to him every year, but he did all these things in a cold, formal way. It had been especially hard to talk to him in the last year because all his father could think about was Ida and Walter and money. The Westphal estate was large but it needed some rebuilding, and the Consul had been asked to lend money for that. If the money was not paid back before his death, it could be taken out of Ida's inheritance. He talked about this constantly, and Otto had to discuss certain banking and inheritance laws with him over and over again.

Sitting on the train going toward Ballenstedt, Otto promised himself he would not talk about money this time. There were more important things. War had come, and he might be killed. He was not going to die without putting all anger and bitterness behind him. He would tell his father that he respected him and was grateful for his training and his faithfulness. His father could believe him or not, just as he preferred.

The first person he met was Max, who was on his way back from the post office with a six-month supply of stamps for his mother. He looked fine—fresh and happy and excited about the war—and when Otto told him that it probably wouldn't last more than a few months he was disappointed. His regiment was going east, where they didn't expect much fighting at first anyway, and he was afraid that the war might be over before he even heard any gunfire.

Otto went to see his mother first, but only long enough to tell her that he was home and well and would have to leave in a day and a half. Then he walked to the other end of the house to see his father. There was no use putting it off until evening, or saving what he had to say for their farewell.

The Consul was at his desk looking at a letter and making notes for his reply. (He always made notes before he wrote a letter, and he had taught his sons to do the same.) He looked very well. His short white beard was trim and shiny, and his cheeks were a healthy pink. They shook hands, and Otto told him that he was on his way to Oldenburg. Then, as quickly and calmly as he could, he said that he wanted to be reconciled to him, that he was thankful for the constant care he had been given while he was growing up, and that he would always profit from the many good habits which he had learned from him. "Whatever may have come between us in the last years, I want to put it away," he said. "With the world as it is, there should be no distance between a good father and his son."

This speech caught his father off guard, and he pretended to be surprised that Otto thought there had ever been any trouble between them. It was a father's duty, he said, to show his sons the right way and point out their errors, even when it was painful to do so, and that's all there was to it. Hard feelings and difficulties should never be allowed to come from such a *natural* thing. However, if Otto had some ill feeling, then it was a good thing to lay it to rest.

Otto was not fooled by his father's innocent talk, but it didn't bother him, either. He had not, after all, come to make his father apologize to him. He just listened while his father discussed "a father's duties," and then let him change the subject.

They talked about the war. What about the reservists? All those bakers and trolley-car conductors and hotel managers and lawyers who were now wearing uniforms, were they ready to fight a war on two fronts? Otto nodded. Yes, at least the reservists in his unit, both officers and line soldiers, would perform well. His father smiled. They talked about horses, and the geography of the Western Front. The Consul sent for coffee, and they talked together until dinner. They even laughed, bitterly, about the wisdom of having Austrians and Hungarians for allies. Otto felt right. He had done what he had to do. He had taken full responsibility for letting Trude go. That's what being reconciled to his father had really meant. And it was true. It was *his* loyalty, *his* obedience, *his* fear that had made him let her go. The blame was his, and now he had taken it. The record was set straight, and he was free and ready to go to war.

The next day he rode over to Wedderstedt with Max and his mother. (The Kiep family was the first one in Ballenstedt to own an automobile—there were now five in town—and the only one with a chauffeur.) He knew Ida needed to see him. He was her brother, but more important than that, he was her friend.

She was almost speechless for a few minutes after they arrived. Walter had left to join his regiment in Halberstadt the day before, and she felt abandoned. "Oh, it's so good to see you," she kept saying over and over again. After a good lunch Otto said, "Come on, we'll go see Walter. Halberstadt isn't such a long drive, and Fritz needs the practice." At first Ida was afraid. "We'll never find Walter among all those other soldiers," she said. Otto shook his head. "The easiest thing in the world," he said. "Get your hat." Ten minutes later they were on the road. The fields on both sides were a deep, rich green, and as they rolled along at twenty miles an hour it was hard to believe that Germany was at war, and that fields just like these were already being spattered red with blood.

They talked about the house at 4 Hughenden Terrace. Ida remembered it exactly, even where all the different dishes were kept. It was still, for her, the *ideal* house, the perfect place for a child to grow up. There was a deep open well and well house in the back yard, and every few days during the spring one of the boys had to go and pump it out. She had gotten her finger caught in the pump one afternoon after school and screamed and screamed until Otto came and set her free. From then on they called the pump the Dragon, and the pump house the Dragon's Cave. Ida had always been the Princess, and for a while Otto called himself The-Knight-of-the-Princess-of-the-Very-Wet-Cave.

It had been a beautiful time, Otto said, but this was a beautiful time, too. The war would not last long. It was caused by ignorant politicians in London, Petersburg, and Rome, but no nation could support a modern war for long, and the best-prepared nation was all the more likely to win.

When they got to Halberstadt, Otto found Walter easily and the three of them went to the White Horse Restaurant for coffee. He had never seen Walter in his uniform before. He looked very good. His narrow, sensitive face and the dark, elegant officer's uniform went well together. The two men discussed the war and Walter agreed that it would last only a few weeks, and that Ida had little to worry about.

Still, Otto said, if Walter was captured or delayed at the front, Ida ought to have a paper that would permit her to draw money from the bank and do what had to be done with the property until he got back. Walter immediately saw the sense of this, so Otto got a piece of paper from the waiter and wrote out a short "power of attorney" certificate, which Walter signed. Then they went for a long walk together and had dinner before Walter returned to his quarters, and Otto and Ida rode back to Wedderstedt.

Otto left early the next morning, going first to Hanover, where there was a delay because of the sudden increase in the number of trains moving west, and arrived in Oldenburg a little after eleven on the evening of August 3. The passenger platforms were crowded with military equipment, and extra lights had been strung out into the railroad yard to permit night crews to unload and sort cargo. The air was warm, and it smelled of horses.

The headquarters of the Sixth Reserve Dragoon Regiment was twenty minutes away from the station, but it was a good night for a walk. He passed eight or ten groups of soldiers on the way, who saluted very smartly and pleasantly, and he decided that summer was a much better time to start a war than winter.

Men and horses kept arriving for the next three days, and it took three days more to outfit and divide the horses, organize and pack the wagons, and turn the regiment into a somewhat workable military force. The chief,

Oberstleutnant von Rüxleben, had commanded the cavalry school in Hanover, and considered it a curse to have been given a regiment made up of "nothing but reservists and civilian horses."

The worst part of those first days was that Otto's hands got terribly sore. He had been used to working with pens and paper. Leather and horses were something else. His right hand, particularly, got red and swollen, and he couldn't get a glove on over it. It was two weeks before the swelling went away, and a month before his hands were tough enough.

Otto was assigned to the Third Squadron under Rittmeister Andersen, and as the youngest officer in the troop had to bring up the rear. He was given a young horse hardly broken to the saddle, but at least it was strong and not nervous. The regiment crossed the Belgian border on August 14 behind General von Bülow's Second Army. Still the war did not seem real to him, and he half expected to be told one morning that it had been called off and he must march back to Germany immediately, being very polite to all the Belgians he met on the way. He passed through Charleroi after the battle for the bridges was over, and there for the first time he saw large numbers of dead soldiers, his own and the enemy's. East of Charleroi, at Namur, he was shot at for the first time. But it was from a distance, while he was on patrol, and none of his men were hurt.

A week after that, on a two-man patrol, he was almost killed.

He and a sergeant named Schneider were on a road which ran east from St. Quentin, where a big battle was beginning. They rode through a wooded place, and when they came out into the sun again they suddenly found themselves within range of a line of French soldiers on their left. The French saw them immediately, and seven or eight of them fired off their rifles. Schneider was hit in the neck and chest and the force of the bullets pitched him over onto the ground like a stone. One of the last shots in the volley killed Otto's horse, which fell on its right side, pinning his leg. There were a few more shots, and then silence. So, he said to himself, it's over. I'm caught. He had a sword and a pistol but he had no intention of using them. The enemy had him in its hands and that was that.

After a minute he looked cautiously over the side of the dead horse and saw two French soldiers with bayonets on their rifles coming down the hill. Another soldier shouted down after them, "If they aren't dead yet, kill them."

When they were about twenty yards away, Otto called out to them in French, "My comrade is badly wounded and needs medical help, and I am caught under my horse. We are your prisoners." The two soldiers stopped, surprised to hear French, and the taller one said something to the shorter one that Otto couldn't make out. Then they came closer.

He spoke to them again. "I'm pinned under my horse. We are your prisoners. My friend is badly wounded and needs medical attention."

"We're going to kill you, you German pig," the taller one said, glancing for a moment at his friend.

"Why? We can't harm you."

"Because you Germans are doing it, and you officers are the most responsible ones."

Otto shook his head. He was determined to make this into a civilized conversation between serious men in search of truth and justice. It was his only chance. "Stories like that go around in every war," he said. "I assure you, as a fellow soldier, that we are not killing French wounded."

The tall man took a step toward him. "You're lying," he said. Over the man's shoulder Otto saw a sergeant start down from the French line. "I'm sure that French officers have not ordered their men to kill wounded," he said. "It's against the rules of war."

"So is starting a war," the shorter soldier said. "What are you doing in Belgium?"

Otto ignored this. "If we soldiers do not act like gentlemen, there will be nothing left of honor," he said.

The sergeant reached them now. He was about thirty years old, and probably also a reservist. A terrible look passed over the tall private's face. Otto could see what he was thinking—that he should never have started talking to this German pig, that he should have shot both of them right away. The sergeant looked at Schneider. "Your comrade is seriously wounded," he said. "Are you?"

"My knee is hurt where the horse fell on it, but otherwise I'm all right," Otto said. He was wonderfully relieved. He would not be shot. It came to him how ridiculous he must look pinned down under a dead horse, talking French. "We were talking about shooting prisoners and wounded," he said.

"Oh? Have you an opinion about that?" the sergeant asked, sounding exactly like a schoolteacher. (Otto found out later that he *was* a schoolteacher, from a small town on the Loire River.)

"In these circumstances," Otto said, "an opinion is forced on me. If your men were to shoot me, and German soldiers found me here, they would probably guess what had happened, and do the same thing to some French wounded, and it would go on back and forth like that until all the lies we told about each other came true."

The sergeant shook his head. "You, or your soldiers . . ." he said, but then he stopped and walked around to see how much of Otto's leg was under the horse. "We'll see if we can lift your animal off your leg," he said, "and take you to Guise. There may be a doctor there for your comrade. May I please have your gun and sword?"

They got the horse off him, and he found that his knee was bruised but not twisted. He pretended that it was very painful and that he could hardly walk on it, knowing that if the French retreated from St. Quentin they would either have to find space for him in a wagon or leave him behind. He and Schneider were sent to Guise in a hay wagon, and when they got there Schneider was put with a few French wounded in one house and he was put under guard in another. They fed him a good dinner, and that night, when the order came to retreat, they left him behind. The next morning German troops entered the town and he was free again.

He got back to his regiment at La Fère a day later. Everyone was surprised to see him. Stories had been going around that the French were shooting wounded and prisoners, and they thought he was dead. Andersen, his squadron chief, shared some brandy with him, and even Oberstleutnant von Rüxleben seemed happy to see him again.

Mail had come, including a letter from Klaus with some newspaper clippings. They were three weeks old, but he read them all once and then read some of them a second time. It was like getting news from another world, impossibly far away. Most of the clippings had to do with events in Berlin. At half past noon on August 4 all the deputies of the Reichstag had attended a religious service at the cathedral and then marched in procession to the White Hall of the Palace. Chancellor Bethmann-Hollweg, in the uniform of a dragoon officer, sat to the right of the Kaiser's throne with all the ministers of his government. To the left of the throne sat the generals and admirals. When the Kaiser stood before the throne to deliver his speech he was wearing a gray army uniform. He was greeted by applause and cheers, and read his speech in a serious, strong tone of voice. At the end he handed his speech to the Chancellor and continued in a raised voice, "From this day on, I recognize no parties, but only Germans. If the party leaders agree with me on this matter, I invite them to step forward and confirm it with a handshake." The leaders of the conservative parties, the Center, the National Liberals, and the Progressives, went forward quickly and gave him their hands, and the assembly, carried away with enthusiasm, shouted and cheered. Men wept tears of joy at this display of national unity. Everyone seemed ready to offer his life for the future of Germany.

Which seemed absolutely right to Otto, but terribly far away, and a little unreal.

He folded the clippings and put them away in his

leather briefcase. He imagined the scene in the great White Hall. It made him proud of his country. *Now was the time for Germany to be one nation.* The Kaiser—a foolish man in some ways, it had to be admitted, vain and petty and easily carried away—was in this moment absolutely right. It was no time for separate parties, for socialists and conservatives and nationalists and moderates. It was a time for unity, and no honorable German could fail to offer the Kaiser his hand.

The army kept advancing through Laon, Vailly, Coulonges, Verneuil, and across the Marne River to Montmirail. From there on the third of September he was sent south on a long patrol to see which French units were moving toward the front. Traveling by way of Morsains, he reached Villiers St. Georges, southeast of Paris. On the way he saw a few French army units, none of them large. (One of those units saw him, too, but he was too far away for them to catch him.) Then the roads began to fill up with troops and artillery, which were coming not only from the south but from the east and west as well. He was suddenly in great danger of being captured or killed.

He rode north as hard as he could and arrived late at night at the corps headquarters in a barn near Vauxchamps. It was full of older officers studying maps, hearing reports, and discussing possibilities—working their way slowly toward a major decision about the way the war would go. Should they drive ahead for Paris, and risk being cut off by the French, or should they withdraw to fortifications to the north and east? He made his report to a cavalry major and was then given a cup of beef soup

and some bread and shown to a table out of the way of
things where he could rest and eat and watch. He was
very tired. He had been on active duty now for a little
over a month. It felt like a year.

During the summer of 1912 he had read a book called
The Great Illusion, by Norman Angell. It proved that no
nation could fight a modern war for very long. It was too
expensive. Modern industrial states depended so much
upon one another that they would run out of money and
raw materials in a few months. And when such a war was
over, the winner would be just as poor as the loser, and
no safer than he had been when it began. War, then,
which had always been immoral, was now also insane.

But how many people believed that? Did the officers in
this barn believe it? Certainly not. They believed exactly
the opposite, that victory was absolutely good and defeat
absolutely evil, and that war, though not good, was a
necessary tool for solving the present problem. And in his
heart, so did Otto. Germany *must* have the victory. It was
worth dying for.

So, in spite of Angell's theories, the war might not be
short. If the generals decided not to strike for Paris but to
retreat to forts and trenches and hold out until the
enemy asked for peace, it might last a long time. And if
the enemy also went into forts and trenches with the same
idea, and if the people back home kept believing in their
soldiers and believing in victory, the war could go on for
years and years. And everybody, even Max, would get
enough fighting.

The decision was made to retreat to fortifications north
and east and get ready for the French and British, who
were preparing major attacks with fresh troops. The re-

treat was quick and orderly, and by the time the enemy attacks came, the new line was strong. Unable to break through, the British and French dug in, and the front became fixed. By the end of October, the line was so hard that Otto's cavalry regiment was withdrawn. He was ordered to remain near the front, however, at the General Staff Headquarters. He spent a lot of time questioning French and British prisoners. (The British soldiers were always amazed at being questioned by a Scotsman wearing a German uniform.) He also took shorthand minutes of staff meetings and copied conversations passing along the open telephone line connecting all the units in the sector.

Time passed quickly. In November there were heavy rains and everyone talked more about the cold than about enemy guns. At headquarters, life was comfortable. Otto had a warm room in a large and beautiful house a short walk from the headquarters building, and he enjoyed working with his fellow officers.

Christmas came. There were packages and letters from his mother and father, and from Klaus, Louis, Max, and Ida. Louis sent him an excellent leather wallet, which he used for the next fifteen years. There was a midnight service and singing around a Christmas tree in the headquarters building. Long after midnight he went to his room and wrote a poem to send to his mother and father, and when that was done he went out alone and walked down the frozen road, thinking and remembering.

He knew exactly how far the nearest British soldiers were, and he wished that they were closer, for just this one night, so he could hear them sing. English Christmas carols belonged to him, too.

VIII

Mixed Duties

On December 18, Oberstleutnant von Rüxleben sent a letter to the staff headquarters asking that Reserve Lieutenant Kiep be returned to his cavalry regiment as soon as possible. The headquarters adjutant replied politely that Reserve Lieutenant Kiep's services would continue to be needed for an indefinite period of time. Otto was delighted. He liked life at headquarters. It was less dangerous than the front and less boring than a cavalry station behind the lines. There were always new things to do and new people to meet, and the food was better.

At the same time he felt that he had deserted his friends, and that bothered him.

In January he got a week's leave to go to Berlin for his final law exam. He still kept his apartment at Tempelhofer Ufer 19, and he spent two days there eating bread and cheese, drinking coffee, and studying. The exam was hard, but he passed. As he was leaving the hall, he met Berndt Solmsen, who had gone to school with him at Ilfeld and was now a submarine officer. They went for dinner together at the Black Piggy, and spent the evening eating oysters, drinking German champagne, and talking.

Berndt was married now and had a one-year-old son. Just before leaving home, he had written a letter to Principal Mücke reserving a place for his son in the Untertertia class of 1927.

"An excellent idea, don't you think?"

Otto agreed that it was an excellent idea.

Berndt told him everything he knew about the sea war, which wasn't much. He was sure that German submarines would "break the back of the English navy in eighteen months." Otto smiled. Everyone seemed to know exactly how many weeks or months the war was going to take. Eighteen months was the longest estimate he had heard so far.

The next morning he walked all the way out to Grunewald Park and back, just to see how the city felt. Berlin wasn't as gray and grim as it had been on the first and second of August. He heard some laughter, and saw old and middle-aged men going off to work very cheerfully. People smiled at him—a few said good morning—and quite a few schoolboys, seeing his officer's uniform, saluted him as he walked by. It felt good.

He took a late-afternoon train back to the front.

In February the headquarters moved east to Montaigue and he was given the extra job of organizing parties for the Second Division staff and their guests. There were at least three parties a week, usually in honor of visiting officers and politicians, some with dinner and some without, some with music and some without, some with girls and some without. Most of the parties were held in a low, one-story brick building that was called "Cookhole #2."

He enjoyed arranging parties, but it made him realize how alone he was. He had his family, of course, and a few good friends, but he was still a single man, twenty-eight years old, living alone, with no job except war, no permanent place in the world, no wife to love, and no sons to plan for. It was a good thing for a soldier not to be married, to feel completely free to do whatever he was ordered to do without worrying about a wife and children at home, but it was lonely.

The little free time he had he spent reading letters and newspapers. He couldn't stay interested in a book. For the first time in his life, the novels of Theodor Fontane bored him. He got letters from his mother every four or five days, and they were always interesting. She had a lot of Berlin friends with whom she kept up a lively correspondence, and she sent him all the interesting news and gossip. As always, her political judgments made sense. Even when she was wrong about something, she was wrong in an interesting way.

"The major party leaders are hopeful that the war will be ended on good terms by early 1916," she wrote in March. "This seems to me too hopeful." A few people were predicting that the United States would come into the war, but this possibility was not taken seriously. And America would never be a major military power. That, at least, is what the experts seemed to think.

The only thing people seemed really worried about was food. The system that had been set up to keep the civilian population fed was always on the point of breaking down, and estimates of how much food was on hand, how much was expected at the next harvest, and how much would be needed in the next month or year were always changing.

The war also was giving a lot of otherwise intelligent people strange ideas. An idea was being discussed by certain important Berlin ladies to destroy all the Italian art in Germany. This, it was said, would discourage people from visiting Italy, and that in turn would lead to Italy's economic collapse because, *as everybody knew*, the Italians depended upon tourist money to live. A number of his mother's friends took this idea very seriously. "If they can't find better things to do than cook up such schemes," she wrote, "they should be sent to the front to play checkers with the wounded and wash dishes."

The important thing was for intelligent Germans to see the situation as it really was.

Even if the Russian government agreed to end the war, which it might do out of fear of revolution, the French would say no. And if the French agreed, which they might do if Paris was taken, the English wouldn't. It was completely ridiculous to hope that the English would give up by 1916, and she couldn't understand how anyone who knew anything at all about British life and British politics could think that they would.

Sometimes he thought about Trude Köhn, who was now Trude von Bismarck. He spent one long evening in June telling Dr. Hübner, the chief medical officer of the division, about her and the circle of men and women and children who had picnics and parties together, took long walks in the summer along the shore of the East Sea, and danced on the lawn at Cladow. He would never meet anyone like Trude again, he said. After this terrible war

there would be no such women left. The new generation
of young virgins would be far different from the generation that had grown up before 1914.

In June the staff went to Hungary, where they set
up headquarters for an offensive into Serbia. The Austrians and Hungarians had been throwing themselves
against the Serbs for almost a year without getting anywhere. Now was the time to nail down the southern
corner of Europe against the Russians and open the
Orient Railway between Germany and Turkey. The
offensive started in October, and by the end of November
the key Serbian cities had been taken by a mixed force of
German, Austrian, Hungarian, and Bulgarian troops. By
mid-December the campaign was over. Part of the staff,
including Otto, left Serbia by train on December 17, and
arrived in Charleville on Christmas Eve.

Otto was given a brief leave and went home to Ballenstedt for two days, where they celebrated an "extra
Christmas" in his honor, and to Wedderstedt for two days
more. In Wedderstedt he saw Dorothea, his new godchild, and celebrated Christmas again. On January 3,
1916, he was back on the Western Front. An offensive
was being planned in the area of Verdun.

The offensive began on February 21 and went on for
seven bloody months. By the end of March an advance of
two hundred yards was being spoken of as if it were a
major victory. A single farm became the objective of a
whole week of fighting, and two days after it was won, it
would be lost again. The shelling was so constant and
heavy that telephone lines were cut as soon as they were

laid. Otto suggested the use of carrier pigeons, and was given the job of organizing them. With a corporal to help him, he made sure that a cage of trained pigeons went along on every attack to carry messages and maps back to the headquarters at Fort Douaumont. Four to six minutes after the bird was released at the front, he was in his cage and Otto had the message—an artillery barrage was needed, the French had taken or given up a hill, a new mine field had been laid in front of a grove of trees, an ammunition carrier had been lost.

As the wet and filthy spring dragged on, Otto was asked more and more to question British prisoners. The aim was to get information as quickly as possible. Most of the prisoners were trench soldiers—privates or lower-rank officers—and the information they could give was useless if it wasn't fresh. A trench soldier would know what his own unit was doing at the moment—whether it was entering the line or leaving, whether losses were being replaced, and how well supplied it was—and perhaps he would have a reliable rumor about what the units on his left and right were doing. That was the most he would know, and two or three days after he was captured, he rarely had anything of value to tell.

In some sectors there were stories of prisoners being tortured and killed. Otto never saw it, but he heard the rumors, especially about what the enemy was doing. He was not surprised. He remembered how close he had come to being shot at the beginning of the war, when nerves were fresh and before horror stories about German "atrocities" had a chance to grow and blossom in the enemy countries.

He read a pamphlet taken from a British corporal that

told about German troops in Belgium bayoneting children and boiling their bodies for soup. Certainly there was a French translation, and possibly a Russian one, too. People wanted to believe stories like that. It gave them an excuse for doing whatever they felt they had to do to win the war.

Otto always questioned prisoners in his office, with the door closed and a guard outside and no weapons anywhere in sight. He offered tea and fruit, and he tried to keep a conversation going. He acted like his father when he talked to timber buyers—asking questions, making suggestions, finding out in a friendly, business-like way what he wanted to know. He usually didn't get any useful information, but once in a while he was lucky. One afternoon a British artillery captain boasted about the accuracy of his gunners, and to prove it gave the location of the difficult "blind spot" from which they had to shoot. Otto gave him a piece of paper, and he drew a map!

Aside from the satisfaction of getting information and the pleasure of speaking English, questioning prisoners reminded him that his enemies were human beings.

Verdun was a butcher shop through which good and brave men were pushed every day. Bodies and nerves were torn and destroyed. "There are men here who will beat their children because of what this battle has done to them," Dr. Hübner said to Otto one night. "For nothing! If only Germany would get a real victory out of it, it would not be so hard to bear."

At the end of April, Otto started waking up at two-thirty or three in the morning. He would get out of bed, go quietly down the hall, and step out onto a narrow stone balcony in the east wall of the fort. There he would do exercises to relax and stay warm and get his mind off the battle. Then he would go down to the kitchen and eat something, and go back to bed around four. When he woke up at six he usually felt fine—ready to work a twelve- or fourteen-hour day.

Early in June, three people let Otto in on the "highly secret" information that General Kosch was going to be sent south again for an offensive against Rumania. Kosch was a fair and diligent, a sensible and brave man. Otto went to him and asked to be taken along, and Kosch told him that he was already on the staff list. "Verdun is no place for either one of us," he said.

A few days before Otto was to leave, while he was describing his duties to another officer, Louis suddenly appeared. He had been in Berlin on naval business, and was on his way back north. He looked in excellent health and he was full of enthusiasm, so his visit was a very happy surprise. For one thing, it gave Otto a chance to show him that he was using his Christmas wallet.

They sat over coffee and brandy and talked about how the war was going. "A strong peace is in our grasp," Louis said, "and not by the submarine alone. Certainly it will play an absolutely vital part, but we also have the best cruisers afloat." Admiral von Capelle had told him that Germany was putting two new submarines into the water every week. The Admiral had estimated that the war would be over by the spring of 1917 *at the latest.*

Louis began talking about engines, armor plate, guns, and torpedoes, and Otto sat back and listened, glad that his brother knew as much as he did about the technical side of ships, and enjoying the fact that he sounded the same in 1916 as he had twenty years before—successful, aggressive, and young—a bright boy trying to sound like a banker.

While they were talking, an officer whom Otto knew only slightly came over and stood near the table. "Do you know that you're both speaking English?" he asked after a few minutes. Otto nodded and introduced him to Louis. "We've always spoken English. We grew up in Scotland. It's the language of our childhood."

"You sound like two spies."

Otto smiled. "Two very stupid spies," he said.

The officer shrugged his shoulders. Speaking English, he said, could get them into a lot of trouble in some places. The German people, it had to be remembered, were at war with the English. The English were, one might say, the *premier* enemy, and some people might think it at the least very unpatriotic to use their language. Certainly, no true German could speak English nowadays with pleasure.

Otto shrugged and tried not to appear angry. Germany, he said, would some day have to speak with the British as well as the French and the Russians, and then it would be in her interest to have as many Germans as possible speaking those languages well.

The officer shook his head. "When the war is over," he said, "the wise Englishman will speak German." He smiled at Louis, told him what a pleasure it had been to meet him, and walked away. Otto watched him go.

"She's gane like Alexander/To spread her conquests farther," he said, quoting Robert Burns.

Louis was embarrassed. "I didn't even realize we were speaking English," he said.

"Neither did I," Otto said. "It's a bad thing when a man has to pretend he only knows one language. Verdun is making us all foolish."

He left for the south on the sixteenth of September. Of his friends from the Verdun staff only two, Major Schumann, who was Kosch's adjutant, and Dr. Hübner, came with him. The three men called themselves the "Verdun Remnant." Kosch's force was made up of two German divisions, three Turkish and three Bulgarian divisions, an Austro-Hungarian brigade, and a mixed fleet of small boats on the Donau River.

The campaign began in October, moved quickly, and by the end of the year the important Rumanian objectives had been taken. In the middle of January the staff moved into a row of very comfortable and warm houses in the city of Brăila. They didn't know how long they were going to stay, but they expected it might be a year or more. Otto was given the job of producing a newspaper. An excellent British-made printing press had been found in the basement of the city hall. "It deserves to be used," Kosch said. On April 1 the first issue of the *Donau Army Newspaper* came out, with German in the left-hand column and Rumanian in the right, so that the civilian population could read it. In June a second newspaper, in Turkish, Hungarian, and Bulgarian, was added. Otto had never done any newspaper work before, and it took almost all his time, but it was a satisfaction.

In September 1917, after nine months as a newspaper editor, he was asked to do some law work. The mayor and the harbormaster of Brăila had been arrested for spying, and he was appointed to defend them. The headquarters of the Russian army was only five kilometers away, on the other side of the Donau River. The two men were accused of sending messages to the Russians by means of bottles dropped in the river.

The first thing he did, even before he saw his clients, was to send a soldier in a rowboat out into the middle of the river to drop in five bottles of different sizes and shapes. Meanwhile, Otto went down the river as far as he dared and watched for them with a pair of binoculars. Soon he saw all five floating along together not far from the enemy side of the river. Clearly it would be quite easy for the harbormaster to receive notes from the mayor, seal them in bottles, and send them to the Russians in this way.

He went to see the two men. They claimed to be innocent, and to prefer the German army to the Russian army, though they admitted that they would be happy to see both armies go away. Otto wasn't sure whether he believed them or not. But that didn't matter, really. The question was, how much evidence did the Army Field Police have?

When the trial began, it became clear that the army had no real evidence at all. There were two witnesses, both policemen, who swore that they had seen the harbormaster and the mayor "talking daily," and that the mayor sometimes gave the harbormaster papers, which he took with him on his boat. Three times, it was testified,

the harbormaster was seen "dropping objects that appeared to be bottles" over the side of his boat.
That was all. That was their whole case.

When the prosecution was finished, Otto called three witnesses to testify to the good character of his clients. Then he questioned the harbormaster. Did he and the mayor talk often? Yes, the harbormaster said, they talked almost daily on matters of harbor business. Otto showed him a folder of papers—permits, reports, and so on—which the mayor had given him over the past few months. Were they all harmless and routine papers? Yes.

Then Otto asked the final, necessary question: "Have you at any time, for any reason, attempted to communicate with enemies of the German Reich?"

"No, sir, I have not."

"The charges put against you in this proceeding are, then, not true?"

"They are not true."

Otto then called the mayor, and put him through the same set of questions. One of the three judges asked the mayor to explain certain papers, which he did. He was very nervous, but his answers were simple and convincing. The case was then over. The prosecutor made his summary, repeating the charges of the Army Police, and Otto pointed out the lack of evidence against them. "No German court holding to the standards of German law could find defendants guilty against whom there is so little evidence," he said.

The judges deliberated for about ten minutes and set the two men free. They were amazed. The mayor kept shaking Otto's hand and wouldn't let go. Both men had been sure that they were going to hang, and now they were free. Suddenly, Otto was the hero of the town. People stopped him on the street to shake his hand and talk, which was pleasant but also a little embarrassing. After all, he was a German officer defending men who might have been guilty of helping Germany's enemies. He was glad the thing was over.

But it wasn't over. The case was reopened by the prosecutor's office and the two men were arrested again. This time a bench of five judges heard the case. Otto's defense was exactly what it had been the first time, and so was the decision: not guilty because of insufficient evidence. This time the mayor did not shake Otto's hand so long. He was more angry and afraid, now, than he was grateful and happy. And this time no one came up to Otto in the street and shook his hand.

Two days later the men were arrested again, without Otto being told, and taken to Bucharest for a third trial. After a three-hour trial, they were found guilty and sentenced to death. The mayor's wife stayed in Bucharest to see if she could find a German lawyer there, and the harbormaster's wife rushed back to Brăila to see Otto. She told him what had happened and he went to see General Kosch right away. It was likely that the two men would be hung in a hurry, so there was no time to waste. Kosch knew the case, and he was shocked to hear that it had been taken to trial a third time in another army district. Such a thing could not be tolerated, he said. It was an insult to the courts and officers and judges of the Donau army.

He told Otto to draft a letter to Field Marshall Mackensen, outlining the case and asking him to intervene. Otto wrote it out immediately, Kosch signed it, and it was sent that afternoon. Mackensen didn't want to take sides in such a small matter, so he compromised. He let the guilty verdict stand, but changed the sentence to life in prison. In the circumstances, this amounted to a pardon. A peace treaty with the Rumanians was being worked out, and when it was signed, most political prisoners would be set free. At most, the two men would have to spend a year in prison.

Both wives were delighted and grateful, and Otto felt satisfied. Winning the first two times had been easy. He had never really had to make a case for his clients. It had been enough to point out how weak, how really impossible, the opposition case was. This time he *had* made a case, by connecting his "unimportant" clients with the pride of the Donau army. In this way he had saved the lives of two possibly innocent men.

That night he took a walk through the city. He was proud of himself. He had "stood for the good habits and character of the German people." He had demonstrated the value of German faithfulness and persistence. (The police, sad to say, had demonstrated the *dangers* of German persistence.) He suddenly felt completely at home in Brăila, even though he was far away from everyone in his family, and didn't really enjoy speaking Rumanian very much.

A week later a delegation of citizens came to his office and gave him a beautiful cigarette case with his initials on it. He kept the case until 1938, when, by accident, he left it on a table in a London restaurant. When he returned for it, it was gone.

IX

Russia

In the fall of 1917, revolution broke out in Russia. The Eastern Front immediately began to collapse. Entire divisions of the Russian army started dropping out of the line. "Either you get us home," they told their officers, "or we will shoot you and get home on our own."

Taking advantage of this collapse, 200,000 German soldiers moved east through Bessarabia, crossing the old Russian defense line almost without a shot. Germany was desperate for food because of the British "hunger blockade," and southern Russia was said to hold great stores of wheat.

In the west, a few units of the French army had threatened to go on strike, and the entire Sixteenth Army Corps was crippled by mutiny. All over Europe, the cry for "socialism, bread, and peace" was growing. Politicians in the Western capitals were becoming nervous. What had happened in Russia might also happen at home. Perhaps they ought to end the war before the workers and soldiers got together and did it by themselves. Revolution did not seem likely, but it had not seemed likely to the Tsar, either, and now the Tsar was a prisoner of the Bolsheviks. Some said he was already dead.

So the tide began to run for peace, and the generals and admirals and cabinet ministers in Berlin, Paris, and London dreamed of one more victory, one last reason for patriotic joy, before it was all over.

The Brăila headquarters was dissolved, and the Donau army joined the move toward the Ukraine. Austro-Hungarian units, no longer under German command, were moving the same way, and the German divisions sprawled across the country in a rush to reach the Black Sea ports first. Otto was part of the forward command which was to take the surrender of Odessa, occupy its public buildings, and hold on until the rest of the army caught up.

All the way there they kept passing through German-speaking towns and villages where the people built their houses and planted and harvested their grain in the German way, and thought of themselves as completely and absolutely German, even though many of their families had been in Russia for five or six generations. They welcomed the German troops as saviors, and it was sad to have to hurry through such towns, stopping only long enough to greet the mayor, pick up some bread and cheese, and check out the map.

On March 15 they reached Odessa, a big, dirty shipyard city that had just been abandoned by the Bolsheviks, many of whom were Russian army soldiers who had gone over to the revolutionary side. On the twenty-first a trainload of soldiers and a small headquarters staff went up the coast to surprise Nikolaev. A captain led the group, and Otto was his second in command. When they got there the city was quiet, and nobody paid any attention to them. The shipyard workers, who were well armed, held the harbor area, and it was decided to leave them alone until help came. The key buildings were occupied—the radio station, the power plant, the water-pumping station, the police station, the city hall, and the central hotel.

On the morning of the twenty-third a trainload of reinforcements arrived, and the captain went to meet them. Twenty minutes later the shipyard workers boiled up from the harbor and attacked the German centers. Before long they had captured the city hall and the radio station, and the hotel was surrounded.

Otto ordered all the doors and windows barricaded. (On the east side of the building, where the dining room was, there were large windows only five or six feet above the sidewalk.) Before the barricades were up, bullets started coming in the windows and two men had been wounded. The workers apparently were well supplied with guns and ammunition. Were they willing to burn the hotel down even though the Russian staff was still in it? (The cooks and waiters and maids and clerks had all reported for work that morning, and were now huddled together in the kitchen.) If they were, the battle was lost, because they could easily throw fire bombs from nearby roofs. Otto sent some men to break through the cellar floor and fill bedspreads with dirt to throw on gasoline or kerosene fires, one bedspreadful for each window, downstairs and up.

The second day, the attackers thought to cut off the

water and electricity. But they never threw fire bombs. The third day, the twenty-fifth, more German soldiers arrived by train from Odessa and the siege ended. The workers simply disappeared, and the firing stopped. By that time three more men had been hurt, two by bullets and one by flying glass. The captain of the relief troop told Otto that a German army doctor had come on the train and was now at the hospital. He had the wounded put on a horse-drawn laundry wagon and went there with them.

The hospital was crowded with wounded, half of them Russians and half Germans, many still on stretchers on the floor. Otto found a Russian doctor and asked him, first in bad Russian and then in good French, where the new German doctor was. He didn't know, and pointed upstairs. Otto started toward the staircase and suddenly saw Max at the end of a little side corridor, lying on a high old bed that seemed to be mounted on bicycle wheels. He was pale and unshaven, and dressed in a hospital gown. Otto went over, took his hand, and leaned close to him. "Brambles?" he said quietly, using a name he had given Max when he was a boy. Max opened his eyes and grabbed Otto's hand with both his hands. Otto asked him if he had been shot. He shook his head and smiled. "Stuck," he said, and then he quickly told his story.

He had arrived with the first relief force on the twenty-third, and gone with a small squad to the radio station. They were attacked there just a few minutes after they arrived. Workers rushed into the station shooting in every direction. He was stabbed in the abdomen with a bayonet and immediately fell down and pretended to be dead. After the attackers left, a Russian sailor found him and brought him to the hospital.

Otto listened to his story, nodded, and told him that he no longer had to worry about anything. He was halfway to Ballenstedt already, where he would get a genuine Kiep super-cure. Then Otto left him and went upstairs to find the German army doctor. He wasn't there. He had gone, by mistake, to the small hospital at the Russian Orthodox Monastery. He didn't get to the city hospital for another hour. By then Russian doctors and nurses had taken care of all of Otto's wounded.

He was exhausted when he got back to the hotel—he had not slept for three days—and found a man waiting there for him, Pierre Kazantski, a welder at the shipyard. He had come to discuss (in very good French) "certain matters of interest to the workers." He and his comrades were ready to clear the docks and harbor, he said, beginning immediately. Food and coal were in very short supply, and the workers would accept, for a brief time, "a fair wage to be paid promptly in goods."

His suggestion was excellent, Otto said, and was in keeping with the temporary nature of the present German occupation. The army did not intend to hold the city forever, and he was sure that arrangements for payment in food and other supplies could easily be worked out. "Our action in southern Russia has been forced upon us by the British hunger-blockade and the entrance of America into the war," he said. Germany had come to Nikolaev only in order to survive, and would be able to leave the city as soon as peace came.

Mr. Kazantski listened politely, nodding every once in a while. He knew the German problem well, he said, because he spent all his spare time reading history and economics. And, in the light of his broad private study, he had another proposal to make. The German government should now declare that the shipyards were German property. Then, when the war was over, the government could turn the shipyards over to the workers "in some suitable ceremony, with all the proper papers," and the workers would get their rights without having to go through the Russian revolutionary government, which would be busy with other things.

It was a crazy idea, which made Otto like it, but it was also a sad idea, because it assumed that the Germans could do anything they wanted to do—wipe out ownership, cancel debts, create a new system of justice—remake the world according to their own ideas.

Otto told him that no military authority could do what he was asking. Kazantski didn't believe him. He looked down at the floor and shook his head. "If you can get your army all the way from Berlin to Nikolaev," he said, "you can do anything you want to do." Otto decided not to argue this point, and asked him what would happen if the workers did get control of the shipyards. Kazantski shrugged. There would be problems, certainly. It would not be easy for the workers to run things by themselves. Germans were *born* knowing how to manage things, but Russians were not. Only Russian grandmothers knew how to manage everything, and everybody in Russia was not a grandmother. Still, it would all work out. A few of the wrong people would be shot, and some people who should be shot would get by, but everything would work out in time, and the new managers would prove to be better than the old ones.

Otto tried not to look surprised, but it was hard. Here was a pleasant, friendly man looking forward to the day when he could line up "the people's enemies" and shoot them down for the sake of justice and good management. Mr. Kazantski put his hand on Otto's knee. "Nothing new has ever happened in the world until now," he said, and he somehow sounded happy and hateful at the same time.

Otto promised to telegraph Kazantski's proposal to the headquarters in Odessa, and to let him know their answer immediately. Mr. Kazantski, on his part, promised to organize the clearing of the docks on Otto's word that the workers would be paid. They had a drink of vodka, and then another, and then a third, and Kazantski left.

Otto sat alone for a long time. So, this was the "New Soviet Man." He imagined Nero watching Rome burn and saying, as he took out his violin, "Nothing new has ever happened in the world until now."

During the next two weeks, until he had made arrangements for Max to go home on a hospital train, he had the pleasure of seeing him for two hours every afternoon. It was a real joy. They talked about the past and made plans for the future, and Otto told crazy stories. "Do you know why the doctor wasn't here the day I found you?" he asked Max one afternoon.

Max smiled, lay back against his pillow, and said no, he didn't.

"Ah, my dear Max," Otto said, looking up at the ceiling and puckering his lips, "it is a long, sad, and beautiful story. Shall I tell it to you, long, sad, and beautiful as it is?"

Max nodded and Otto, looking even sadder, began. It seems, he said, that the doctor had been "born a skeptic in matters of religion." Even as a young child he had despised going to church, refusing to move when his mother called him to put on his little coat and go with her to divine services. All the other boys in the neighborhood grew more pious and holy as they got older, but Hermann—for that was the doctor's name—only grew more vain and worldly. When he was eleven, he started wearing a false moustache, which stuck out seventeen centimeters on each side of his face, and putting glycerin drops in his eyes to make them look bright and shiny.

When he was eighteen he decided to become a doctor, and while he was studying at the university he continued to become more and more vain. During anatomy class, while they were examining a corpse, he would sometimes raise his hand and say, "Dear Professor Doctor, don't you think that I have a better-looking body than that corpse does?"

Finally he got to be a doctor, and the war came, and he went into the army, and was sent to Russia, and then to Nikolaev. When he got to Nikolaev he asked to be taken to the hospital, but by accident he was taken instead to a Russian Orthodox monastery. When he got there and looked around and saw the monks with their beautiful beards and lovely brown eyes full of religious joy, he immediately decided to devote his life to God and never to leave the holy grounds of the monastery until his beard was at least a meter and a half long. Fortunately, however, as he was hugging one of his new brothers he discovered that the man was wearing a false beard, a thick face wig of bear fur. He immediately spat on the floor and left the place in disgust, hurrying to the real hospital and vowing to devote his life, from that moment on, to medicine, ugliness, and atheism. His goal in life now was to become the ugliest atheist doctor in Europe.

Two days later, Max asked him to tell him the story again.

Otto stayed in Nikolaev until the end of April, and then went farther east to join the headquarters staff in Simferopol. During his time in Nikolaev he worked in a small living room/office on the second floor of the hotel setting up a newspaper. On April 24 a Protestant pastor, Emmanuel Winkler, came to see him there.

He had heard of Otto from the mayor of a small German town near Odessa. "Lieutenant Kiep," the mayor had told him, "is a true German officer, and the model of an English gentleman." This combination, Winkler said, had made him curious. He was now on his way to Simferopol, hoping to get a pass to travel throughout the Crimea and renew contacts with German colonists which had been broken by the war. He also wanted to urge the military authorities to offer transportation and travel papers to those Germans in occupied Russia who wanted to return to Germany when the German troops withdrew.

Who, Winkler asked, would be the best man in Simferopol to discuss these things with? Otto immediately wrote him a letter of introduction to General Kosch. When that was done, they talked for a while about the beauties of southern Russia, ate some German crackers with Russian cheese, and drank a little wine. Just before Winkler left he told Otto that he now understood what the mayor had meant. They promised to see each other again.

From that time on, Otto began thinking less and less about war and more and more about peace. What would happen to the Crimean Germans when the war was over? If Germany was forced to accept hard terms, what would happen to the Russian and Hungarian and Rumanian Germans? Would they lose their property, or be driven out, or killed? How much revenge would the French demand for a four-year war fought on their territory? And more important than anything else, what would have to be done to win back the unity and power which Bismarck had given to Germany?

Questions, questions, questions.

No answers.

Long before the capture of Odessa it had been decided in Berlin to set up an independent Crimean Republic under German protection. It was a foolish and cruel thing to do. An independent Crimea would never be able to stand against Russia once the German army was gone. The Crimean Germans, especially those who had joined the new government, would have to leave or face Russian revenge. They loved the Crimea. They had farmed it and made it beautiful. Why should they leave their barns to the Bolsheviks and go back to Germany, where people were starving? Germany was their nation, certainly, but Russia was their country.

A few weeks after meeting Winkler, Otto was transferred to the headquarters in Simferopol. He tried to meet as many Crimean Germans as he could and put them in touch with higher-ranking staff officers he thought might be sympathetic with them. He had an excellent assistant at the newspaper, a young lieutenant from Marburg, and as soon as the first issue of *German Newspaper for Crimea and the Taurien* was out he asked to be assigned to do liaison work between the army and the German community in the Crimea.

This job put him in close touch with Winkler, and he grew to like him more and more. Winkler was a very ambitious man, but his ambition was entirely at the service of what he called his "Russian parish." Outside of it, importance or power didn't mean anything to him. Somehow he stayed intensely Christian and intensely nationalistic at the same time.

The summer went by quickly, and the war situation on the "other front" grew worse. Field Marshal Ludendorff, who had been called by some Germans "another von Moltke," had lost his magic. The army in the west was failing, and more American troops were entering the line every day. Peace was coming by way of defeat.

In October, Otto went to Berlin. He had made friends with a number of officials in the new Crimean government, especially the Trade Minister, Rapp, and wanted to support Rapp's plan for new money credits for Crimean banks. Louis, who was now on the staff of the naval headquarters, met him at the train. What he said about the condition of the navy was shocking, but not surprising.

"We haven't a single ship we can trust entirely, not

from the smallest to the largest," he said. "Everywhere we are only one step from mutiny."

A mood of defeat and bitterness was everywhere. You could sit in a café and watch the people walk by and know that the war was lost.

His appointment at the Foreign Office in the Wilhelmstrasse was for eleven o'clock. He went at nine to the cathedral and just sat inside for a while thinking. Then he walked in the direction of the Kaiser's Palace. Along this street in August 1914 the Reichstag deputies had walked on their way to hear the Kaiser's speech and give him their hands and hearts.

"From this day on, I recognize no parties, but only Germans."

Now it had come to this—a beautiful October day in a city full of tired, badly fed, and mostly bitter people. The enemy had at last brought together enough men and guns and food to defeat Germany and be her judge. It was as simple as that. This terrible war, which was every country's guilt and every country's insanity, would be blamed on Germany alone, and she would be made to pay the price.

Before he left the Foreign Office that afternoon, he had been offered a job in the diplomatic service. It came as a complete surprise. He said he would think it over.

X

Versailles

Otto arrived back in Berlin on the afternoon of Tuesday, December 24. Winkler was with him, and as the train clicked across the switches outside the station, they stood by the window and finished eating the bread and sausage they had bought in Brest-Litovsk three days before. The first thing he did when they got off the train was to send a telegram to Ballenstedt telling his parents that he was home and wishing them a happy Christmas. He sent the same telegram to Ida in Wedderstedt, and then he and Winkler went to find a cab.

There weren't many cabs, and none of them would take them to Otto's apartment at Tempelhofer Ufer 19. One driver told them that a group of Spartacists had blocked streets in that part of the city and even fired machine guns at the police. Was there fighting going on there *now,* Winkler asked. The cab driver didn't know, but a taxicab had been turned over and burned on Saturday, and stores broken into.

They decided to walk. They had both spent a lot of time with armed workers in the past few months, and didn't feel afraid. Besides, this was Germany, not Russia, and an officer's uniform still counted for something, though perhaps not very much.

Halfway home, when it was already starting to get dark, they decided to go into a restaurant to warm up and have a beer or a cup of coffee. The place they went into was empty, and before they sat down, the owner came over to say that he was very sorry but he had neither beer nor coffee. He had been promised beer for Friday, but of course, with the way things were, who could tell whether he would get it even then? And coffee? Who had that? However, his guests should not despair. For an officer of the army who wore the "true Iron Cross" (Otto had received the Iron Cross, first class, after his defense of the headquarters in Nikolaev), he would make coffee from his own small supply. Otto protested that that would not be proper or acceptable, but the owner insisted.

Otto thanked him, and they sat back down and waited.

A German restaurant with no beer. Otto could hardly believe it. The Communists didn't worry him, but a disillusioned people whose government could not guarantee them a glass of beer or a cup of coffee on Christmas Eve, a people who felt like victims not only of their enemies but also of their leaders, could be terribly dangerous.

The coffee came, and a plate of milk chocolate which had been cut into small pieces and neatly arranged. After the owner put them down he stepped back from the table and said, in a low voice, "I am still loyal." It was a touching thing, and it made Otto feel both sad and hopeful. The Kaiser had deserted Germany in November, fleeing to Holland, but German loyalty had not fled with him.

A block from his apartment the street was barricaded. Part of the barricade was a trolley car that had been taken off its tracks and turned around. A few men were standing around a bonfire in the middle of the street, and a man of about fifty was standing in the trolley-car door with a rifle on his shoulder. He told them very politely that he was a representative of the "People's Vanguard of the Berlin Soviet." As such, he required them to show him their identification papers.

Otto told him, in an equally polite way, that he and his friend would *exchange* papers with him if he wished. This the man was willing to do, so the three of them passed their papers around. When the guard saw that both men had just come from Russia, he wanted to know what it was like there. Had either of them seen Lenin or Trotsky or any other famous revolutionary? Was it a peaceful and happy country?

"In the Crimea," Otto said, "it was very peaceful and happy. But the Russians did not rule the Crimea. The Germans ruled."

The man shrugged, smiled, and let them through. The next day the barricade had been moved somewhere else, and the only sign of the Berlin Soviet was a round black spot on the street where the bonfire had been.

On the twenty-seventh, Otto left Berlin again for a short visit to Ballenstedt. Max was still there, happy and almost completely recovered from his wound. Otto spent a lot of time talking politics with his mother. As usual, she saw things clearly. "There will be no peace conference," she said. "They will simply bring in their surrender books, and we will have to sign them. We will be lucky to come out with enough potatoes to eat."

He returned to Berlin on the fourth of January and immediately reported for work at the Foreign Office. During the next few weeks they moved him from desk to desk, getting him acquainted. Winkler was also at the Wilhelmstrasse, trying to smooth the way for German refugees coming from the Crimea and elsewhere. Both men were terribly busy, full of new experiences, and in spite of the desperation and hunger of Germany, very hopeful for the future.

In April, Otto was posted to the peace conference, and went to Versailles. The German delegation was large—over two hundred—and his job was to work with those parts of the treaty that had to do with German citizens and property in foreign countries. After a few days he began to do some translation too. The official translators were experts in language but not in law, and to translate certain things properly one needed to be both. He began by helping with a sentence or two, and was soon spending days and nights at it. (To do the same thing for the French texts, a German lawyer with a practice in Brussels was brought in.)

The weeks in Versailles were terrible. The German delegates were kept behind fences all the time. A narrow walkway went between the hotel and the conference building. Every morning Frenchmen lined up on both sides of it to shout at the Germans as they went from the hotel to their work.

As a kind of private protest, some members of the delegation refused to drink the French wine that was offered at meals. Otto did not join them. "Punishing my stomach will not cause the French delegation to get indigestion," he said. The large table at which he ate became known as the "Tasters' Table." No matter how difficult and troublesome the day's work had been, the men at the Tasters' Table ate and drank and laughed. One Friday, after an excellent trout, Otto went to see the cook. His mother's great-grandfather, Jean François le Goulon, had been a French cook and was the author of several cookbooks. The hotel cook did not recognize the name, but he was delighted to be compared with him anyway. After that visit, the Tasters' Table would get a German dish every three or four days. It was the only kindness shown to them during their stay in Versailles.

The terms of the treaty were unbelievably and mindlessly hard. Germany was to give up an eighth of her land, a quarter of her coal fields, and three-quarters of her iron and zinc. Eupen, Malmedy, and Moresnet were to go to Belgium, and the Saar to France for fifteen years, along with the disputed territory of Alsace-Lorraine. All the German colonies overseas had to go, too. It was clear almost from the beginning that no important provisions were going to be changed. For every small concession the British, French, and Americans made, there were dozens of refusals to reconsider a case or make an exception.

One person dominated the whole scene, even when he wasn't present: Georges Clemenceau, Premier of France. He was determined to have his revenge. He would have his adjustments and reparations and punishments. He would win for his country, now that the chance had come, the leadership of Europe. And if Europe itself should suffer for this, well, let the Germans take the blame for that, too.

After weeks of meetings, consultations, and the exchange of notes, Clemenceau let it be known that he was running out of patience. The Germans would have to sign or face occupation. So the delegates gathered their papers and traveled to Weimar, where a new German parliament was waiting for them. It was a parliament unaccustomed to power, brought together by the force of disaster to make peace and prevent civil war. It was not up to such a task. The oldest congress in the world would not have been.

The delegates from Versailles, including Otto, tried to persuade parliament to reject the treaty. It was, he said to everyone he met, "completely unacceptable." But not to agree to it was also completely unacceptable. It meant that the enemy would march to Berlin and oversee the breakup of the nation. Signing the treaty meant saying, in effect, "Yes, we are the criminals of Europe," but refusing to sign meant turning Germany into a colony of France and England.

The deadline was June 23. The parliament debated, heard brave speeches of defiance and despair, and finally voted to accept.

The delegation immediately resigned.

In July, Otto took ten days off and went to Scotland and England. He had a number of good reasons for going. First, the Foreign Office was encouraging its members to travel to former enemy countries and make personal contacts. Second, his father still owned half of the timber firm in Glasgow. The business had to be looked into, and a way found to transfer some of its assets to his father's bank account in Germany. Third, he wanted to be in Scotland again. He had been cut off from it for four years and he wanted to take advantage of his new freedom to go there.

He arrived in Glasgow on a gray, chilly, miserable day. It was wonderful to be back, to be a Scotsman again, to walk along the Great Western Road and ride on top of the two-decker trolley along St. Vincent's Street. The people in the Kiep office and the men at the shed remembered him as a friend and no one, as far as he could tell, held back because he had fought with the "Huns" during the war. He went to see a friend at the Bank of Scotland, got the necessary papers as well as some good advice on transferring money from Britain to Germany, and visited the Hillhead School.

He had a cousin living just outside of London, and he wrote from Glasgow telling him he was in Britain. The cousin's wife replied that they were very busy with guests at the moment but that he would be "most welcome to drop in." Her letter was somewhat chilly, but he went anyway.

There was a party the afternoon he arrived, and his cousin insisted that he join it. Guests wandered around the garden sipping sherry and talking. His cousin introduced him to some people, and he let it be known that he had spent the last four years in the German army. This knowledge made people feel uncomfortable, as if some large, strange, plant-eating beetle had just flown into the garden. Still, they behaved as they had been taught to behave, politely, like Englishmen.

They moved from the garden to the drawing room to get out of the evening chill, and then on to the dining room. They sat down. Soup came. It was very good. A man sitting opposite him in a British officer's uniform said it was excellent.

Otto took a deep breath and agreed.

Meat came, and a lady at the end of the table commented that it, too, was excellent.

Otto took a deep breath, and agreed, adding that it was, however, not as good as baby.

"Baby what?" a gentleman asked.

"Baby person," Otto replied.

The table became absolutely silent. "What do you mean by *that?*" the same gentleman asked.

Otto acted surprised by the man's question. Certainly, he said, everyone in the room had read articles and pamphlets during the war telling how German soldiers enjoyed eating babies in soup, fried, broiled, and boiled.

Nobody around the table said anything. Then the officer opposite him smiled. "You are remembering Jonathan Swift," he said.

Otto shook his head. "No, Jonathan Swift was a great writer, and a great politician, and an honor to Britain," he said. "I am remembering certain hack writers who make up lies in time of war in order to create public hatred for the enemy, and then, when peace comes, even good men find the lies hard to forget."

Again there was silence, but it was the silence of thought. In their minds these people were still at war with Germany, but they were perhaps a little less ready now to believe *all* the horror stories about the beastly Huns.

After dinner the men went to the library for cigars and brandy, and the women went upstairs to talk and probably have a little something to drink too. During the war Otto had fallen into the habit of standing with one hand on his side, German-officer style. It was the way the Kaiser often stood, and Hindenburg, too. (The Kaiser's son, the Crown Prince, had a more relaxed style. He liked to lean against doorways looking detached and superior.) This way of standing was the one habit Otto deliberately tried to change since joining the diplomatic service, so when he was offered a chair he took it and let the victors pose before the fireplace.

He was asked what he thought of the Versailles Treaty. There was no point in being anything but honest and direct. "All of Europe, and here of course one must include Great Britain, will suffer from it. It will make German democracy a hard thing to float. At its *best* it is merely bad economics; at its worst, it is the millstone that will carry us all down."

XI

Winning a Point

On the second of March 1920, Otto was sent to the German Legation in The Hague, Holland. The Minister in The Hague was Dr. Friedrich Rosen, and Otto served him as Legation Secretary. Rosen, who later became German Foreign Minister, was a man of remarkable abilities and wide interests. He taught Otto what diplomacy was, and how it should be carried on. "Learn what the other side *has* to have, and what it merely *wants* to have or *desires* to have," he said, "and know the same about yourself."

He helped Otto to see, by his understanding of politics, his insight into people, and his capacity for self-criticism, what a humane task diplomacy can be.

Rosen was certainly different from Emmanuel Winkler. He knew more. He had wider interests and a broader political view. He was also more patient. Winkler was a nationalist, while Rosen knew that to serve Germany you had to serve Europe. But in some ways the two men were alike. They both had a strong sense of responsibility, enthusiasm, generosity, and the freedom which comes from not being afraid.

Every morning Otto and Rosen got together in Rosen's office and looked at the day's work. Otto had been sent to him as a kind of apprentice, and Rosen would take the time to give him the political and cultural background of every important question. It was like studying under a master teacher. The only thing Rosen didn't know, or have a feeling for, was economics, and there Otto could contribute a certain amount of expert knowledge.

Two or three times a week they took a walk together, and Rosen would lecture on one of his interests. He was an expert in Persian culture, had written a Persian grammar book, and was doing a translation of the works of Omar Khayyám.

In Holland, Germans were treated like human beings. Holland had been neutral during the war, and the Dutch hadn't learned to hate either side. If anything, they were a little pro-German. The food was good, there was a tradition of elegant parties at the embassy, and one of the best men there, Gesandtschaftsrat von Reisswitz, had both a charming wife and a great cook.

As a result of going to diplomatic parties and eating in good restaurants, Otto gained over thirty pounds in six months.

After a year at The Hague the German Foreign Minister, Dr. Simons, asked Otto to travel to London with him as his private secretary. Negotiations were beginning on reparations. How much was Germany going to pay, to whom, in what form (cash, goods, credits, raw materials?), and when? Simons remembered how useful Otto's knowledge of the English language and English law had been at Versailles, and someone had told him that he knew shorthand. His job would be to read the English documents, copy and translate the English speeches, and keep Simons up on the state of English public opinion.

On March 2, in a speech at Lancaster House, Simons told the Allied delegates that Germany was not negotiating on the basis of her "war guilt." He recognized, he said, that Germany was required to pay reparations and would have to find a way to do it, but she did so because of her obligations under the Versailles Treaty, not because she considered herself a "war criminal."

The British and French hit the ceiling. The arrogant Germans, the immoral Germans, the shameless and uncivilized Germans were forgetting that they had lost the war. To the British in particular it was vital that Germany admit her guilt. British law demands that a victor *show cause* before he can take something from the person he has defeated. Either there is a material cause (the enemy has destroyed your property) or there is a moral cause (the enemy has committed a crime). The British and French demands under the Versailles Treaty were based upon a moral cause, which was written into the treaty as Article 231:

> The Allied and Associated Governments affirm and Germany accepts the responsibility of Germany and her allies for causing all the loss and damage to which the Allied and Associated Governments and their nationals have been subjected as a consequence of the war imposed upon them by the aggression of Germany and her allies.

Simons tried to hold his ground, but it was impossible. World opinion, backed by the military power of the Allies, would not accept the "arrogant posture" of the

German Foreign Minister. Pressure was put on the government in Berlin, and a new cabinet was formed in which Rosen replaced Simons as Foreign Minister. As further punishment for Simons's defiance, French and Belgian troops occupied Düsseldorf, Duisburg, and Ruhrort. This act, it was said, would teach Germany a lesson and make her easier to deal with in the future.

Shortly after Rosen left The Hague, he asked Otto to join him in Berlin. He planned to reorganize the Foreign Office from the ground up, and Otto was to assist him in the personnel department. After less than two months, however, it became clear that Rosen lacked the energy for the job. He was a diplomat and a philosopher, not an organizer or decision-maker. He had been away from Berlin for many years, and he was out of touch with the members of the Reichstag and the political parties. He soon became the target of plots within the department and in the press. The Chancellor, Joseph Wirth, didn't understand Rosen or his plans and gave him no support. As a result, he asserted himself less and less and after a few months dropped his plan for reorganization entirely.

He was soon asked to resign as Foreign Minister, and Walther Rathenau took his place. Before Rosen left, he wrote a letter of recommendation for Otto's file. He sent a carbon copy of it to Otto with a little note on top: "For your information/F.R." The letter read, in part,

Dr. Kiep is an extraordinarily able, thorough, and well-informed official. I can, without any fear of overstatement, testify to his outstanding capacity for diplomatic service. Dr. Kiep combines an extremely lucid, natural intelligence with superior legal training. His dedication to his chosen field, international law, does not in any way narrow him or limit his scope. On the contrary, his healthy judgment and good sense always keep his attention on what is purposeful and realistic. His perfect understanding of the Service makes it unnecessary to speak of diligence and conscientiousness. His efforts are always directed to the progress of the job at hand, without any personal distractions. His good health allows him, fortunately, to accomplish unusually large amounts of work.

Perhaps Rosen couldn't run a government office, but he certainly knew how to praise a man.

Rosen's absence gave Otto a few weeks to clear up his desk, visit his family, and rest. He invited Klaus to come to Berlin and they spent a week together going to the theater, talking, and visiting friends from the old Berlin circle. The last evening Klaus was with him they had dinner with Walter Gropius, who was now a very well known architect, and laughed with him over the famous party at which Gropius had played bullfighter and Otto and Klaus were park-bench lovers.

When Klaus was gone Otto called up Illi Grisson, Ida's Berlin friend. Illi loved him, and they had kept in touch through the years. Now she was a teacher, and it made him feel good to know that her simplicity and honor and intelligence were at the service of children.

He picked her up after school and they went to Kempinski's Restaurant for coffee and cake. They talked for two hours about family and politics. She was skeptical about everything connected with politics, and everyone in the government except Otto. She believed in hard work, intelligence, and loyalty. "We are alike," Otto said to her. "We both still believe in the things we believed in when you were twelve and I was eighteen."

He got her home much later than he had expected to, but neither of them minded. It was the most satisfactory time he had spent with a woman in over ten years.

On May 16, 1922, Otto was sent as deputy to Prince Fürstenberg-Stammheim, the ambassador in Budapest. The Prince was not a very lively man, but he had a good heart, and when he saw that Otto was intelligent and responsible he set him free to do things in his own way. During their weekly "work conference" Otto would outline problems and suggest courses of action. The ambassador would listen, approve most of Otto's suggestions, and ask him to carry them out.

Otto had a cousin living in Budapest, Bessie von Szenzö, who welcomed him and made him part of her family circle. He knew the countryside from the war, and liked it very much. The man whose place he was taking—Gesandtschaftsrat von Tiedemann—had a beautiful apartment overlooking the river, and within a few days Otto felt completely at home there. After a few weeks he began to use the language.

Aside from the ambassador, the men he got to know best were Hungarian-Germans, among them a professor at the university, Jacob Bleyer, and an attorney named Max Gündich. Both men were committed to protecting the rights of the German minority in Hungary, seeing to it that they were not discriminated against, that their churches and newspapers were kept alive, and that their citizenship rights were not violated. It wasn't easy. The Hungarian government was not interested in the German cause. Hungary had fought on Germany's side during the war, and now blamed Germany for the loss of it. From the official Hungarian viewpoint, everybody who was born in Hungary and entered her life was Hungarian, and to feel a loyalty to German culture was a kind of treason. "This is our Hungary," they were saying. "Love it or leave it."

In June 1922 Walther Rathenau, Rosen's successor as Foreign Minister, was shot to death on a Berlin street. The murderers fled to Hungary and were hiding out on the estates of certain leading Hungarian nationalists. When this became known, Chancellor Wirth asked Hungarian Prime Minister Bethlen to see to it that they be arrested and returned to Germany at once. The Prime Minister replied that he would "investigate the matter," and did nothing.

Even if he had wanted to do something, Bethlen didn't have the power. The estate owners who were hiding the fugitives had land, and money, and popular support. Many German political agents living in Hungary also wanted the murderers to remain free. One of them, a man named Scheubner-Richter, who worked for the German National Socialist Party, told Otto at a press reception that the murder of Rathenau was no murder at all, but simply "a direct political act."

"Murder," Otto said to him, "is the end of politics."

"Not at all," Scheubner-Richter said. "It is merely the end of *democratic* politics, and the sooner we end them the better."

Chancellor Wirth's private plea getting nowhere, the German Foreign Office ordered Fürstenberg-Stammheim to *demand* the immediate arrest and return of the murderers. The Prince was away on vacation, and Otto had to handle the matter.

There was no point, as he saw it, in embarrassing a government by publicly asking its prime minister to do something he didn't have the power to do. He went to see the Hungarian Foreign Minister privately and told him about the demand he had received from Berlin. Chancellor Wirth, he said, had taken a personal interest in the matter, and the Foreign Office was pressing the embassy for action. The Minister, an honest and serious-minded man, told Otto that the murderers could not be delivered. It was not a question of good will or bad will, he said. The men were simply out of his government's reach.

Otto thanked him for his honest reply and made a suggestion. If the Hungarian government could make some gesture toward the Hungarian-Germans, something that would please the German public at home, the return of the murderers of Rathenau might become less important.

The Foreign Minister replied that his government *might,* for the sake of its good relationship with Germany, allow the German minority to organize "cultural clubs" if Berlin would agree not to embarrass Budapest by publicly asking for the murderers.

Otto notified Berlin that the Hungarian government was powerless to deliver the murderers, and that, in his opinion, if the present government fell, the next one would be either weaker or more nationalistic. Rather than make enemies, he said, Germany should use the situation to win concessions for the German minorities. The Foreign Office agreed, the surrender demand was withdrawn, and in return the German minority in Hungary received permission to organize. German newspapers, completely unaware of the bargaining which had brought matters to this point, were full of praise for the enlightened attitude of the government in Budapest and the excellent work of the German ambassador and his associates.

This arrangement won for Otto the gratitude of a lot of people, including some he despised. Scheubner-Richter, his fist tight around Otto's elbow, introduced him to some other National Socialists at a party as "my friend, O. C. Kiep," and he received five or six letters of thanks from Hungarian-German landowners who sounded as if they wanted to fight the world war all over again. Still, these were small matters. The important thing at the moment was that he had won for the Hungarian-Germans a right he thought they deserved.

XII

America

I~N~ September 1922, the Foreign Office asked him to go to the United States with the German delegation to the Mixed Claims Commission. Again the issue would be reparations, but the way of working would be different. The Americans were not interested in who was guilty for the war. Certain United States businesses, and some individual citizens, had been hurt by it. The Mixed Claims Commission was to act as a court to which they could bring their complaints. Judgments in every case would be given by an American "umpire," and the German government had agreed to abide by his decision. Otto was to defend German interests on the basis of international law. He wondered how fair the American umpire would be, but he thought the method of working was sensible.

He was just getting to know Budapest, and he was doing good work there, and he didn't really want to get into reparations questions again, but it was a step up in the diplomatic service—he would be given the rank of Legationsrat—and he would be able to use international law in a courtroom setting and would have a chance to get to know America. He had a family reason for wanting to go, too. An ancestor of his, Jacob Leisler, had gone to America around 1660, settled in New York, and made a career in politics and business. He had been one of the first New Yorkers to conspire actively against the British. In time he was arrested and put on trial, and died by hanging in May 1691. After the British were defeated, he became an American hero. Now there was a statue of him in the city of New Rochelle, near New York City. Otto wanted to see it.

He arrived in the United States on October 9, 1922. For the next few months, in spite of a very heavy work load, he tried to meet and talk to as many Americans as possible. The United States had just outlawed the sale or possession of liquor. As a diplomat, he could have as much alcohol as he required, and he found any number of Americans who were delighted to come up to his apartment in the Roosevelt Hotel on Sixteenth Street and have some drinks and talk.

He also spent a good deal of time with Germans who had emigrated to America. Most of them were very different from the Germans he had known in Hungary and Rumania and Russia. They felt at home in America, or at least they didn't feel as if the culture around them were at war with them. Certainly it was true that a lot of Americans thought all Germans were arrogant and stupid and evil, but these were private feelings, private prejudices. The *country* was not anti-German, and as a result the Germans he knew in Washington and Boston and Chicago were more likely to criticize their new country in public, and enjoy it in private, than the Germans he had known in Budapest or Odessa.

The Roosevelt Hotel itself was a lesson in American politics. The clerk on duty from 7 A.M. to 5 P.M. weekdays was sure that every good thing in the world was in the United States, the soul of which was St. Louis. He disliked foreigners, and especially diplomats, and thought they all should be put on boats and sent back home. The night clerk felt the same way about America, but his idea was that America should be the teacher of the world. (By "world" he meant Europe.) The elevator operator had fought in France in the world war. "I did my share," he used to say. Otto never found out exactly what he meant by this, but he could understand the feeling behind it. The night telephone operator was a devout and active Presbyterian woman, with whom he used to talk when he came home late. She was one-fourth German, and she had a lot of recipes from her "wonderful German grandmother."

Otto used to play a game in his mind with these four people. He would think up a problem and then try to find a solution which all of them could agree on.

Problem: Cincinnati is bombed by Eskimos. *The four agree:* Make war on the Eskimos. Teach them a lesson.

Problem: The public finds out that the President, a married man, also has a girlfriend. *The four agree:* He will have to be replaced as soon as possible by someone without a girlfriend, no matter how stupid the man is.

Problem: The German Republic fails, and the nation falls into chaos and despair. *The four agree:* That's Germany's problem. We did our share.

Problem: The Black Plague breaks out in Berlin. *The*

four agree: Send medicines. Send clothing. Send doctors. Organize civilians to kill the plague-carrying rats. Raise the level of medical care in Germany.

Listening to these four people helped him to understand why America had refused to join the League of Nations, and why most Americans didn't care what went on in the rest of the world.

He stayed in Washington for a little over a year, and then in September 1923 he was offered a position on the staff of the Reich Chancellery and returned to Berlin. The Chancellor was Gustav Stresemann, a short, tough-looking man with the hands of a lady and the coolness of a gambler. He had taken office a month before and led a cabinet representing five different political parties. He was courageous and he had clear ideas. His main task, as he saw it, was to end the struggle that was still going on with France and change the politics of war into the politics of peace. This meant getting the French to leave the Ruhr area without making it look like a defeat for them. Before this could happen, certain domestic, "interpolitical" matters had to be taken care of.

Within a few months of taking office Stresemann had broken up a Communist attempt to seize power in Saxony and forced Bavarian authorities to crush an attempt by Adolf Hitler and his National Socialists to create a separate "Bavarian State." (Among those killed in the fighting between police and the National Socialists was Scheubner-Richter, the man who had held Otto's arm in Budapest and called him "my friend, O. C. Kiep.")

On the Reich Chancellery staff Otto worked harder

than he had ever worked in his life, and saw more. It was like being at headquarters during the first day or two of an important battle, when no one knows how it will turn out, and new problems force new decisions every hour, any one of which could lead to defeat.

His job was to advise the cabinet in matters concerning reparations and international economics, and to "assist in other matters as required." German money was breaking down faster and faster every day. In September when he landed in Hamburg, Otto had seen his first million-mark bill, with which he could buy what five marks could buy in 1918. Now in November a billion-mark bill was worth a single 1918 mark. No one wanted to sell anything. It got so bad that the Minister for Food, Dr. Luther, ordered the arrest of grain-mill owners who refused to sell their flour.

Otto hardly ever came home before one or two in the morning, and he had to be in his office at nine at the latest. Often he would come home so tired and with his nerves so worn that he couldn't sleep. He would go to bed and lie there for an hour and then get up and get an apple, and read, or write a letter, or walk quietly around his apartment thinking and trying to plan out the next day's work.

During these frantic months something began to happen to him that he was too busy to notice. He began to open his heart to the possibility that he might, after all, marry. He came to see that he needed a woman to give his life balance and form.

Women had always been an important part of his life, ever since he bought Ida her first hair ribbon. In the last years he had been very close to several beautiful and interesting women. He had spent weekends with them, gone to the theater and to parties with them, shared a few secrets, and exchanged gifts. But he had always made it clear that he did not have marriage in mind. The women he had chosen were all around thirty, with some experience in the world, and they pretended for him that they were not thinking of marriage, either.

Now he began to be ready in case someone different should appear. He didn't make a clear decision about it, but he opened his inner eyes and waited for a woman he could love completely.

Chancellor Stresemann's Great Coalition broke up at the end of 1923, and a new government was formed under Wilhelm Marx. Stresemann became Foreign Minister, and Luther, the former Food Minister, moved to the post of Finance Minister. Marx was trusted by all the parties except the Communists and the extreme Nationalists, not because of his intelligence or strong will, but because of his dependable character and human purity. He was an extremely modest and undemanding person, and Otto was drawn to him immediately. Under Marx the sense of constant crisis left the Chancellery, and though Otto continued to work two or three nights a week until midnight, he could sleep when he got home.

At Christmas he got a vacation and went home to Ballenstedt. Ida and Walter had four children now—Dorothea, who was Otto's godchild, Elizabeth, Irmgard, and a handsome son named Christoph. Klaus came on the twenty-fifth with his wife Loria, a strong-minded, independent, and interesting woman. Klaus was very proud of her. Louis came with his wife Eugenie and their children, and Max came with his wife Johanna. They sang songs, exchanged presents, put on a play (which Otto wrote and directed) , and above all talked politics.

Many of the people Otto talked politics with in Berlin had no real interest in the future of Germany. They were like clever philosophers sailing on a leaky ship. They sat in their chairs on the top deck and discussed how the ship would sink, and when, and who would end up in which lifeboat.

Political talk in Ballenstedt was more human, and for the most part more intelligent.

"If the Mark can be turned into real money again, and if the reparations question can be rescued from the madhouse," Otto said on New Year's Eve, "Germany could have a republic. Otherwise, we will have either the Communists or the Nationalists standing on our necks." He talked about his return to Berlin in 1918, finding the barricade across the street near his apartment, and exchanging identifications with the polite revolutionary at the barricade. "There have never been many Germans who wanted a Berlin Soviet. A Berlin dictatorship under a man like Hitler is something else. Many more people would welcome it."

The greatest thing about being in Ballenstedt was not the political talk but the children. Several couches full of nieces and nephews called him "Uncle Otto," and for each one he had brought a present. Ida's children were sure that he was one of the most important men in the world. He had lived in America, far across the Atlantic. When they were getting up in the morning, he was just going to bed among the skyscrapers and the Indians. He was a godchild of Bismarck and knew Hindenburg. In America he drank coffee with the President and had his picture in the newspaper. To sit alongside him was to sit where President Harding or Premier Poincaré might have sat.

He told fabulous stories and he often had chocolate in his pockets. He *had* to be a man of miracles, power, and enormous wealth.

Early in June 1924, Chancellor Marx invited him to his office and asked him to come to London for another reparations conference. The world was beginning to change, he said. Poincaré's government had been defeated on May 11, and Herriot was now Premier of France. The Americans were pressing the French and the British to take a new look at Germany's debts and her ability to pay. Prime Minister MacDonald seemed interested in really negotiating, not just giving out terms, and even those who still wanted to punish Germany for her war guilt saw that something had to be done to save her from collapse. Otto would go as Marx's private secretary. His job would be to translate documents, keep an eye on the British newspapers, and do whatever else Marx might want him to do during their week or ten days in London. Otto was delighted. He liked London, and it would be a pleasure to serve Marx.

The conference began on the morning of August 5 in a good spirit. That afternoon Marx and Ramsay MacDonald had a private talk, with Otto translating. It was clear that MacDonald wanted the conference to succeed because he wanted the German Republic to succeed.

When the serious part of the conversation was over, he asked Otto how it was that he spoke English with a Scottish accent, and Otto told him about his Scottish birth and schooling. The Prime Minister had been born in Scotland too—he was planning a vacation there in a week or ten days—and so the two men immediately had a personal touch. Before they left each other, MacDonald told Otto to come and see him any time he thought it would help. It didn't matter how late it was, since he hardly ever got to bed before one in the morning. So several times in the next few days Otto went late at night to 10 Downing Street and sat over whiskey and a pipe discussing special problems and getting advice about how they should be handled.

MacDonald's Secretary of the Exchequer, by far the most intelligent man in the Labour Party group, was Lord Snowden, and he also gave the German delegation every support. At one point, when the German delegation voted to accept a particularly hard part of the so-called Dawes Plan, he objected violently. "If the German delegates agree to this obligation," he said, "they do it only under pressure and against their convictions, because it cannot be lived up to."

Because no one else was there to do it—the Reich Press Chief, Dr. Spiecker, had stayed in Berlin—Otto took over the job of meeting with newspaper reporters after each day's work. First he gave out a "press bulletin," which he wrote and edited with MacDonald's agreement, and then he answered questions. He was the one person best able to do it because he was keeping a complete shorthand "protocol" of all the meetings. Every night, after the parties were over and the final good night had been said, he returned to his hotel room and dictated his protocol to a secretary, who typed it immediately.

The hardest problem facing the conference was the French occupation of the Ruhr. The Germans said it had to be ended before any new agreement could be signed. Herriot was willing to promise privately that French troops would be withdrawn after a year, but he refused to put his promise in writing. Several times the conference almost broke up on this question. On the afternoon of the fifth or sixth day, Otto looked up from his note-taking and noticed that MacDonald had left the hall. He followed him upstairs and found him in his workroom packing the things from his desk. He asked him what was wrong, and MacDonald told him that he was at the end of his nerves and was leaving for Scotland. The conference, he said, had failed.

Otto begged him not to go, referring to hopeful statements Snowden had made that morning, and MacDonald agreed to stay one more day. Otto then went back to the hall and described the situation to his delegation. They asked for a recess until the next morning, and during the night a compromise was worked out.

The conference eased the pressure on Germany a little—very little. For Otto personally, it had been a tremendous success. Certain things had happened which would not have happened without him. He may possibly have saved the conference. At any rate, he arrived back in Berlin tired, grateful, and happy.

XIII

Hanna

IN January 1925, Otto was asked to become the government Press Chief. He took the job because it meant a step up in his career, but he didn't feel easy in his mind about it. The overwork and worry of the last two years had taken a lot of his strength. He was feeling depressed and he wasn't sleeping well. Was his whole life going to be a series of leaps from job to job, with holiday visits to Ballenstedt in between? Was work and worry going to be his only bread until he died?

Still, in spite of his feelings, he had no choice. If he didn't take the job, it would probably go to someone less gifted. The future of Germany depended upon good men staying in government service. There were already too many Germans who "understood politics" and felt proud of themselves for staying out of it.

So in February he began a new schedule in a new office:

8–9:30   Review of the major German newspapers and the Wolff Dispatches from overseas.

9:30–10 '   Conferences with the State Secretary at the

Foreign Office to discuss foreign-policy problems and decisions.

10–11   Press conference at the Reich Chancellery.

11–11:30   Report to the Reich President (first Ebert and then, after April, von Hindenburg).

11:30–12   Staff meeting.

12–12:30   Second press conference.

12:30–1:30   Appointments with special press representatives and others.

1:30–3   Official lunches.

3–4   Letters, staff conferences.

4–   Cabinet meetings, Reichstag meetings, diplomatic dinners, beer evenings, and so forth.

One of the enjoyable things about the job was that it included a car and a chauffeur. Every morning he could ride in style to his office at the Reich Chancellery, and at night when he went out, the car and chauffeur were ready. It made him feel, as he said in a letter to his mother shortly after taking the job, almost like a banker.

One evening in late February he went to a "musical evening" at the home of Mr. and Mrs. von der Groeben on the Nicholsburgerstrasse. He had known Vikki von der Groeben since 1920, and her husband almost as long. There was a large, mixed group of people there to listen to music, drink, eat, and talk. Sitting near him was a beautiful young woman, nineteen or twenty years old. He had seen her once before, in the visitors' gallery at the Reichstag, and he thought from the way she looked at him that she remembered him, too. She had long hair, like Trude Köhn, and the same free, independent look on her face.

She was much more than beautiful.

As he watched her, all his desire for the ideal woman came back to him. She was really still a girl, but he would help her become a woman. She would be his wife. "Now or never," he said to himself. "This one or no one." He knew she wouldn't be easy to win. She probably expected to marry a man ten years older. He was twice that. He was still strong, but there were years of travel and work and war behind him. Sitting near her, he *felt* like a young man, but he certainly no longer *looked* like one.

He had to leave the party early to go somewhere else, but he called Vikki the next morning, before he went to work, to find out what the girl's name was. He had trained himself to remember names, but he hadn't heard hers, or if he had, he had somehow forgotten it. "She and I are going to get married," he said, "so naturally it is important for me to know her name." Vikki told him everything she knew:

1) Her name was Hanna Alves.
2) Her father, Georg Friedrich, was a banker, and her mother was "a very sweet person."
3) She was the oldest of three daughters, and her father's favorite.
4) She had a brother whose first name was also Georg.
5) She was studying law at the University of Berlin.
6) She was not simple, but "completely innocent of the ways of the world."

Otto was delighted to hear all these things, except number 3, and asked Vikki if she would have the two of them at her apartment again.

"Next week sometime?"

Otto consulted his calendar. There was a large party on Monday to which he would have to go. Otherwise there was nothing he couldn't get out of. He told her he would be free from Tuesday on, and wouldn't make any evening appointments until he had heard from her.

He repeated what a lovely party it had been, and she assured him of her desire to help him in every way she could, and they said goodbye. It was a beautiful way to start the day. Hanna Alves was like a sudden, unexpected gift. He would spend as much time with her as his work and her parents would allow. And if he could fool her parents during the first important weeks and months, and see her more than they thought he was seeing her, that would be all right, too.

Other men, friends of the family, her father's business associates, had probably been "in love" with her. But flirting with her father's friends (and no doubt with law students at the university, too) was not the same as being courted by an unmarried, persistent, and completely committed man. He would not be shy about showing her how serious he was, or letting her know that he aimed to marry her, the sooner the better.

He saw her at Vikki's the following Wednesday and asked her if he could drive her home. At first she seemed to say yes, and then she got frightened and said she had made "other arrangements." He suspected that she was lying, but accepted her excuse and suggested that she might want to let him take her home the next time they met. She replied that perhaps that would be very nice.

They met again, by Otto's arrangement, and again she did not allow him to take her home. But they talked, long and seriously. He asked her whose lectures she was attending at the university, and what time they were given. They discussed the strengths and weaknesses of the Berlin law faculty. He impressed her. She impressed him. After a few weeks he was invited to spend an evening with her parents. As he was leaving, he asked her if he could meet her in the park on her way to the university some morning. They could walk through the park and then she could go to her morning lecture and he could go to his office. She said she thought that it might be very nice. In fact, she was delighted by the idea, and he knew it. There was something romantic and just a little sneaky about it that appealed to her.

Walking from the corner of Friedrich-Wilhelm Street to the Brandenburg Gate—with a stop by the goldfish pond—became a regular thing.

This courtship was, for him, new life. Meeting Hanna had not made the government of Germany any simpler or easier to serve, but now everything seemed possible to him. It was clear that Hanna admired him and found him attractive. He was polite, he was "correct," he was interested in everything she thought and felt, no matter how childish, and he respected her. And she couldn't flirt with him as she could with other men. He told her that one morning in early April. They were walking through the park and she made some joke about nature *demanding* love in the spring. "By July," she said, "all spring love boils away and there's nothing left." He nodded. Spring love was like that for a lot of people, he said, but not for him. The seasons did not control his life, and what was awake in him in the spring would not die in the summer. "Understanding that," he said, "I'm sure you would not play with me, or encourage feelings you didn't want me to have."

Otto's greatest problem was her father, who wanted to keep Hanna for himself. By the end of April he was getting suspicious. Why had Hanna suddenly started going to her early-morning lectures? Why did she want to invite old Dr. Kiep to family parties? What possible interest could she have in a thirty-eight-year-old politician from Scotland? It was very strange and very disturbing.

He decided to send her away for a while. She wanted to improve her English, she said. Well, she could go to Oxford and take a course. And her sister Lu could go with her to watch her.

Before she went away, Otto decided to tell her about Trude Köhn. He felt that he owed it to her to tell her about the woman he would have married sixteen years before if he had not been obedient and afraid. So, walking with her one Sunday afternoon in early May, he began talking about Trude. Never before in his life had he praised her more forcefully or clearly. He was not going to say, "Oh, Hanna, this woman was nothing compared to you." He wasn't going to lie, even for the sake of passion, even for the sake of sparing the feelings of the woman he loved. He told her about Trude's honesty and love of life, her great patience and modesty, and his long love for her.

Hanna was hurt, though she tried not to show it. She was hurt and confused and almost crying. "You should have married Trude," she said.

"I'm not sorry," he said, "and I would not have told you this except that I hold the same ideal now that I did then. I'm older, and if anything, my love is deeper."

Hanna went to Oxford with her sister at the beginning of June. One morning about a week before they left, Otto proposed to her next to the goldfish pond in the Tiergarten. She said she couldn't give him an answer right away. Perhaps, after she had been in England for a while, when he came to see her, she would be able to say something. Meanwhile, they could write, but there were to be no promises given or received, and his letters were not to sound too much like the letters of a lover. Her mail might be intercepted somehow, and her father see what he wrote.

He kissed her.

They wrote back and forth almost every day. She was very critical of the British, and at the same time she wanted to let Otto know that she was not a gossip and that she was ready to be instructed.

Just before he came to England to see her, her letters became nervous. One day at the end of July she wrote that she now understood him better than ever before. He was really more English than German. That's why he was *rushing* her the way he was, and why he was on such good terms with British and American press reporters, and why he was *presuming* so much. It wouldn't surprise her, she said, if he had already spread the word in Berlin that they were going to be married. Well, she had not given him permission to do any such thing. If she ever got married she would marry a German, not an Englishman, and if he was an example of the German diplomatic service, well, she felt sorry for Germany!

Her claim that he was really English made him not only nervous but angry. It was a charge he had heard before. Several men in the Foreign Office, jealous of his "hothouse career," had been saying that someone who was so *Anglo-Saxon* couldn't possibly have any understanding for Germany. Now the woman he loved was saying the same thing, and it disturbed him deeply. He immediately wrote a reply, in which he began with compliments for the excellent English of her last letter, and then spoke of his long love for Germany.

. . . how can you say I am more English than German. I will have to tell you a lot about my life, so that you may recognize how German I am and feel, starting with the schooldays in Scotland where all of us brothers were persecuted as "German sausages," to the days in Ilfeld, where I first really got to know Germany and decided to stay always. Then the time with our firm in Glasgow, which I was destined to take over, when I entered into deep conflicts with my father because I wanted to become a German and did not want to remain in Scotland. Finally I prevailed, and could study in Germany, and at twenty-one, as my first independent step in life, I was naturalized in Germany so that I might enter the army. Then the war and, immediately after, demobilization to work for Germany! I disdained opportunities to make a lot of money, because I believed that I had a higher calling in politics. Hanna, this may sound like self-praise, but it is really so . . .

Letters were not enough. He arranged an official trip to Paris from August 20 to 24, and took an unofficial side trip to London on the twenty-fifth. Hanna came down from Oxford with Lu and they met at the Savoy Hotel. He was relieved to find that her way of acting had not changed and that she was as worried about his feelings as he had been about hers. The three of them had lunch together, and then Otto invited them to go for a walk in Hyde Park. Lu pretended that she had some shopping to do so that the two of them could be alone.

Hyde Park was one of Otto's favorite places. There were always people there giving speeches—flat-earth people, who proved their views with quotations from the Bible, Communists urging a British Soviet, converts to Buddhism testifying to it as the only true religion, advocates of new alphabets, and so forth. It was a place where a few people expressed their ideas, and a lot of people learned to be tolerant. The speakers were not bothered by the police, and the listeners were always very polite. If you didn't like what someone said, you could walk away or step back and make a speech of your own. The spirit of Hyde Park was the spirit of English democracy.

This particular day Otto and Hanna did not bother to listen to any of the speeches. He wanted one thing, a promise from Hanna to marry him soon. That was why he was in London. He would not bully her, but he would state his case to her as clearly as he could. He loved her, he respected her, and to some degree he even understood her. The two of them were suited to each other. They were both common-sense people who nevertheless had ideals and hopes. If she was suffering pain now, it was the pain of hesitation and indecision. Once she said yes to him the whole future would change for both of them. Even her relationship with her father would be easier if she and he were standing together.

And he loved her. That had not changed, and it would never change. They stopped on their way across a lawn, he looked at her and asked for an answer.

She said yes, she would marry him. Never had a woman's voice sounded so sweet to him.

The wedding took place on December 14 in the Kaiser Wilhelm (II) Memorial Church. There was a little bit of snow falling—snowflakes on a bridal veil are good luck—and a lot of important people were there.

The music was beautiful, the wedding sermon by Pastor Nithack-Stahn was a model of good sense, the reception was dignified and elegant. None of this mattered to Otto at all. His bride was there—that mattered. The two families were there—that mattered too. And the marriage vows were given and received.

> For this cause shall a man leave his father and mother and cleave to his wife, and they shall be no more twain, but one flesh.

After the ceremony he kissed his mother and shook hands with his father and hugged Klaus. "I'm safe in the harbor," he said.

Why had he chosen her? Certainly not because she was so much like Trude Köhn or any other woman. He had chosen her because he saw in her the material for as much perfection as any human being can have. He believed in the good health of her mind and body and will, and in his power to help her grow, and to grow with her. He married her because he believed absolutely in Otto and Hanna together.

They took a train that night for Genoa, and sailed the next day for two weeks in Egypt.

XIV

Hitler

On January 28, 1927, Wilhelm Marx formed a new cabinet, the fourteenth since the beginning of the Republic. Already in the fall of 1926 he had asked Otto to remain with the new government as Press Chief and Otto had said no. The job was demanding all his time, and he wasn't with Hanna as much as he wanted to be and thought he ought to be. They had a beautiful apartment on the Fasanenstrasse, and he always had to be somewhere else. And a baby was coming. It was time to get himself and Hanna out of Berlin.

Several possibilities came and went. The German steamship line Hapag offered him an excellent job, but it was in Berlin, and it would mean leaving government service. Besides, Louis didn't want him to take it. Louis was a Hapag director now, and Otto would be moving into a world that belonged "by rights" to him. There was a place at the League of Nations in Geneva, but at the last moment it was not offered, and a possibility in London, which also failed. Finally he was offered a post in Washington. He wanted to refuse it at first because it would mean a step down in rank. (He would be going from the position of Ministry Director to that of Embassy Counselor.) Still, he liked Washington, and the salary was good, and it would give him and Hanna a chance to share a new adventure, so on December 28 he accepted an appointment as Counselor to the German embassy in Washington.

Eight days before, at home on the Fasanenstrasse, Hanna had given birth to a son, Nikolaus Friedrich Albrecht. In Germany the custom is to give a child a verse from the Bible at his baptism. For Albrecht, Otto chose a verse from the New Testament: "What does a man gain if he wins the whole world, but loses his own soul?" The baptism took place on January 4, and on the eighth Otto left on the steamship *Bremen* for New York. He would find a place to live and then Hanna and the baby—and possibly Hanna's sister Lu—would follow in April.

He took nine or ten books with him to read on the boat. One of them was a book by Adolf Hitler called *Mein Kampf (My Struggle)*. It was a strange book, a mixture of biography (". . . My heart had always beaten only for a German Reich"), and race hate ("The race question is . . . the key to world history"), and political theory. His political ideas were fascinating and frightening.

> The art of all truly great national leaders has at all times primarily consisted of this: not to divide the attention of a people, but to concentrate that attention on a single enemy.
>
> As soon as the . . . masses see themselves in a battle against too many enemies, they will immediately . . . ask whether it can really be true that everybody else is

wrong, and that only their own people or their own
movement is right. Therefore, a great number of basic-
ally different enemies must always be described as belonging to the same group, so that as far as the mass of
your followers is concerned, the battle is . . . against
a single enemy.

Hitler's political party (he had not created it, but he
was now its leader) was the National Socialist German
Workers' Party. In a national election it would probably
get very few votes, but it was growing, and trying to
divide Germany. The National Socialists on the right,
and the Radical Socialists and Communists on the left,
were determined to make the Republic fail. For every
political question, no matter how trivial, the National
Socialists gave an "answer from the right" and the Radical
Socialists and Communists gave an "answer from the
left." Both held the principle of no compromise. They
were not interested in solutions but in chaos and despair.

The Luther government, for example, had fallen over
the relatively small question of what colors the flag should
have.

The Nationalists, encouraged by President von Hindenburg, had insisted *as a matter of principle* on the
old Imperial colors of black, red, and white. The leftists,
also *as a matter of principle,* had insisted on the new
"republican" colors: black, red, and gold. Luther and his
Foreign Minister, Stresemann, tried to force a compromise, ordering that both flags were to fly on all German
ships, missions, and consulates. This order caused a storm
of protest and ridicule, and as a result Luther was forced
to step down. His order remained, however, and for years

the twin flags flew, to the surprise and puzzlement of foreigners.

Otto arrived at the German embassy in Washington— with its two flags—at the end of January and reported to the ambassador, Ago von Maltzan. Von Maltzan knew Otto and didn't trust him. He thought he was too ambitious. Even so, by the end of March they were working together well. Hanna and Albrecht and Lu arrived in April, and that was wonderful. In July von Maltzan went home to Germany and was killed there in an air crash. Baron von Prittwitz, the former Counselor at the German embassy in Rome, took his place.

In spite of changes at the embassy and a great deal of new work, Otto felt completely at home in Washington. He enjoyed American politics—sincere, funny at times, full of plots and frauds, but confident, free from dangers, young and secure. America was still in many ways a primitive country, and the "American manner" was open to foreigners. He had only to express an interest in something to be shown it and told about it.

Americans enjoyed talking to a German diplomat who sounded like a Scotsman. Scots-German was an American sort of mixture, and he was always being introduced to people who told him that they were half Scottish and half Austrian, or half Irish and half German, or part English and part German and part Indian, or some other such combination.

Part of his happiness came from watching Hanna. She was a great "social success." During a diplomatic reception at the end of their first year, President Coolidge's wife sat on a couch and talked to her for twenty minutes while some of the other diplomatic wives looked on enviously. She was young, she was beautiful, and she had a way of being where things were happening. And, naturally, she attracted men. One night on the way home from a party she talked to him about a man who had spent most of the evening with her. Otto had noticed them together, and told her what he knew about the man. She said that she had been attracted to him.

"Well," Otto said, "we'll have to go and see him. I know where he lives, he keeps late hours, and the sooner you find out what attracts you to him the better." He turned the car around and started driving toward the man's apartment. She told him not to be silly, that she would be far too embarrassed to go up. "I have some business with him anyway," Otto said. "You can sit and watch. You need to know what takes you."

When they got to the address she shook her head. She had lost all her interest in the man, she said, and wanted to go home. Otto believed her, so he started the car again and took her home.

Hanna renewed his hope. By her youth and ambition she gave him a claim to the future. He felt like a good musician with a really first-rate instrument to play. She made him want to become better, to play in such a way that people would praise the instrument and player together. She made him feel free and more complete.

But in the pleasures of his work and his marriage he never stopped thinking of Germany, and it was German far more than American politics that held his attention. More and more the German people were being persuaded that they would have to choose between extreme left and extreme right. He heard this not only from German politicians visiting Washington but also from ordinary German citizens who came to the embassy for help of one kind or another.

A German chemist came to him one day in the spring of 1929 and insisted that the embassy stop immediately the American production of a drug he claimed he had invented. It was his property, he said. He had worked on it for twelve years, and now some American firm in New Jersey was making money on it. The embassy would have to force the authorities in Washington or New Jersey to close the pirates down. Why did the German government have an embassy here if it wasn't to make the Americans do the right thing?

Otto told him that perhaps he really needed a good American patent attorney. He was, after all, a scientist, a man who, as a matter of *honor,* looked into things for himself, or at least located his own experts. If he had a lawyer, he could make a direct assault on the villains in New Jersey.

This idea appealed to the chemist and he accepted it as if it were his own. He then began a speech about the need for Germans to stand up to the world, to assert the superiority of Germany "with blood, if necessary," and to raise German culture and science from the ashes of the "betrayal of 1918." Clearly, he had read *Mein Kampf* and taken it absolutely seriously. He never mentioned National Socialism or Adolf Hitler, but he didn't have to. When he was through he got up very politely, they shook hands, and he left.

When he was gone Otto remembered Pierre Kazantski,

the Bolshevik from the shipyards at Nikolaev. "If you can get your army from Berlin to Nikolaev, you can do anything you want to do," Kazantski had said. The world was full of people who believed that guns could remake everything.

In the summer of 1929 he and Hanna went back to Germany to have their second baby, catch up with things at the Foreign Office, and show off Albrecht. On August 10 a baby girl—Hildegard—was born in a rented house in Berlin-Dahlem.

While they were in Berlin, Otto saw Trude Köhn again. Albrecht was having ear infections and he took him to see Dr. Emil Köhn, Trude's brother. Dr. Köhn had an old nurse who had been with him from the beginning and knew all the family secrets. Her long white nurse's uniform was always starched as stiff as a suit of armor, and she had small, angry-looking blue eyes. She had always been nice to Otto whenever he came in, asking about his health and the health of his "gracious wife."

She told him that his old friend Trude von Bismarck was visiting the doctor with two of her children. Would he like to see her? He said yes, he would, and she brought him to a small room where Trude was waiting. They greeted each other, and he took a chair. She sat with her back straight, in the posture he remembered from sitting beside her at a hundred tables. Her head was turned a little to one side, as if she wanted to give him the clearest possible view of her. She had, of course, changed. She was forty-two years old, a widow trying to raise her children on not very much money and still give them the important things—music, books, religious faith, a little travel, and the university.

The beauty of her face had not changed. Her eyes were still warm and clear, and her face still had that look of wit and hope that he loved. After a few minutes they talked about their families—Hildegard was just a few days old—and then they parted, wishing each other well.

By October the whole family was back in Washington, and at the end of the month the New York stock market crashed. Stocks which had been worth six hundred dollars dropped to two hundred dollars between morning and afternoon, and twenty-four hours later were selling for forty dollars.

Otto's first thought was of what this would do to the German economy. American banks were part of the system through which reparations payments were being made. Suddenly even the greatest American banks were becoming desperate for money. Everyone was calling in loans in order to pay debts. Moneyless debtors who had borrowed on stocks had to forfeit them, but the stocks were now almost worthless. Banks began to fail.

Beyond reparations payments there was the matter of international trade. German businesses dealing in the United States or with Americans were suddenly put under new strains, and some of them broke. American investment in German businesses ceased almost entirely.

Bankers and politicians weren't the only ones hurt. In 1927 there had been over a million Germans without jobs. In 1929 the number jumped to two million. By the end of 1930 there were over three million unemployed.

The number continued to climb, and by 1933 there were more than six million German workers without jobs.

As unemployment grew, so did the membership of the National Socialist Party. In 1928 there were twelve National Socialist deputies in the Reichstag. In 1930 there were a hundred and seven. In 1932, when Otto had moved to New York to begin serving as German Consul General, there were two hundred and thirty. The deeper the troubles, the better it was for Hitler.

The Reichstag was splintered so badly that the important business of government was carried on by presidential decree. The National Socialists called for a new government, a new order, an entirely new *spirit*. Joseph Goebbels, the National Socialist public-relations man, set out to convince the whole nation that every true German had to become a National Socialist and that salvation lay in following the leader, the Führer, Adolf Hitler.

THE TRUE NATIONAL SOCIALIST

What does it mean to be a National Socialist?

To be a National Socialist means nothing but: Fight, Faith, Work, Sacrifice!

What do we National Socialists want for ourselves?

Nothing!

What do we National Socialists want for the creative German people?

Freedom!

What ties us National Socialists together, in this fight for Germany's freedom within and without our borders?

The awareness of belonging to a community of fate, a community imbued with a spirit of radical innovation, a community whose members shall be companions, one to the other, in good times and in bad.

What is the National Socialist password to freedom?

God helps those who help themselves! ! !

On January 30, 1933, Hitler became Chancellor and set about making Germany into a Third Reich. (The First Reich had been Charles the Great's, and the Second Reich had been Kaiser Wilhelm's.) Two days later the Reichstag was told to go home. Three days after that, an "emergency decree" was issued restricting civil rights. On February 5, Communist demonstrations were banned and a Social Democratic newspaper was ordered to stop publication for three days. On February 27 the Reichstag building burned down. Hitler blamed the Communists and got from President Hindenburg an "emergency decree" suspending the basic civil rights guaranteed in the constitution—free speech, free assembly, freedom of the press, freedom from search, everything. On March 10, National Socialists took over all state governments, and on March 24 the Reichstag, called into session at the Potsdam Opera House, passed the "Law for Terminating the Suffering of People and Nation," which gave Hitler the right to make any law he wanted to. Four hundred and forty-one deputies voted for it and ninety-four—the entire Social Democratic delegation—voted against it. Hitler now had his foot pressed on Germany's neck.

The Republic was dead.

XV

Einstein

On March 16, 1933, a dinner was held at the Waldorf-Astoria Hotel in New York in honor of Dr. Albert Einstein, the great German mathematician. The dinner had been planned in December as a way of raising money for the Hebrew University in Palestine and the Jewish Telegraphic Agency. People who had already contributed money, or who might contribute money, were asked to come. In addition, invitations went out in early February to various diplomats and dignitaries.

By the middle of February the character and meaning of the dinner had changed. An anti-Jewish government was in power in Germany, and Einstein had become the symbol not only of modern science but of the persecuted Jewish community. A money-raising dinner had become a *political* dinner.

An invitation to the dinner went, as a matter of course, to Ambassador von Prittwitz in Washington and to Consul General Kiep in New York. Von Prittwitz wrote a polite letter saying that he couldn't come, and expressing the hope that the Consul General in New York would be able to attend. Otto was in Florida at the time, and when he got back to his office on March 6 he found the invitation among the other mail on his desk. To go would mean the end of his work in New York, and possibly the end of his diplomatic career. The Foreign Office would see the dinner as an anti-German rally, another act of the "International Jewish Conspiracy," and he would be looked on as a kind of traitor.

The next day he got a cablegram from Louis. Einstein had planned to go back to Germany on the Hapag ship *New York*. Now, according to Louis, friends were urging him not to travel on a German ship because he wouldn't be safe. Would Otto please get in contact with Einstein and assure him on behalf of Hapag that he would be protected? If he took another ship it would be an insult to Hapag and to his country. Otto replied that he would do what he could, but the cable annoyed him. What ship Einstein went back on seemed to him to be a relatively small question. The real question was whether he would go back to Germany at all.

On the tenth, Otto heard from his friend Dick Emerson, a German-American who had contacts everywhere, that Einstein was not going to go back to Germany but would take a Belgian ship, the *Belgenland,* to Antwerp. This made Einstein an even more dangerous person to be near. Emerson also told Otto that some German students studying at Columbia University were planning to stop Einstein as he tried to board the boat. These same students, or others, might try to prevent him from attending the dinner.

The situation was becoming more complicated every day, but the question facing Otto was very simple—should he stay home, save his job, and serve National Socialism, or should he go and lose his job in the name of German decency? To that question there could be only one answer, but it was a painful answer. It meant ending his work in New York. He wrote to the dinner committee saying that he would come.

He was asked, as the highest-ranking German guest, to give a short speech. He said that he would be glad to. If a man was going to do something that would cost him his career, then he ought to do it in as public a way as possible.

He had told Hanna about the invitation on the day he got it. She understood as quickly as he did what it meant. Why did it have to happen? The dinner was, in itself, a small thing. There was at least one dinner of this sort in New York every week or two. If only Einstein had been unable to come, or the dinner had been held in Montreal! That Otto's career should be wrecked because of it was too much to bear. But of course he would have to do what he knew was right.

Einstein arrived in New York by train at one in the afternoon of the sixteenth. Reporters had sent him a list of questions, and his answers were handed out on the platform. He was asked what his present view of German culture was. His reply was not the kind that would get him friends in Berlin.

Germany's contribution to the culture of mankind is so vital and significant that you cannot imagine the world without it. This must be especially emphasized at the present time when the genuine exponents of this culture are receiving unworthy treatment in their own country . . .

Clearly, the more Einstein spoke, the more dangerous he became.

The dinner was a white-tie affair. The ladies, most of them over fifty, were decked out in elegant dresses. There was a string quartet playing as the guests arrived. Otto found his seat at the head table and tried to relax and enjoy the occasion. He had made his decision, he knew what he was going to say, and he didn't want to waste his time worrying about what would happen tomorrow.

When his time came to speak he praised Einstein for his contributions to science and his service to humanity. Then he thanked the United States for having always welcomed German scholars and scientists. It was the sign of a great nation, he said, to be open to new ideas, and not to judge an idea by the nation from which it came. Then he looked at Dr. Einstein.. "This company does not honor you, Dr. Einstein. On the contrary, you honor this company, and I might say, every company of which you choose to make yourself a part."

The applause that followed was more than just polite. Something true had been said, and most of the people in the room knew it. And a few of them were aware that Consul General Kiep was doing something very hard and very risky.

The next day his speech was reported on the front page of *The New York Times,* and a few days later the Nazi newspaper in Berlin reported that Dr. Otto C. Kiep, an official representative of the German people, had insulted his own country in front of a room full of American Jews.

At the end of April he was called back home for "consultations." He went first to the office of the new head of the personnel section of the Foreign Office,

Prince Waldeck, who was an enthusiastic Nazi. He expected to be told that he was being replaced, but he wasn't. Instead, Waldeck gave a violent speech, in the spirit of the Führer, against all Jews. The true enemies of Germany had finally been named. The true spirit of the German nation and people was now being purified from the poison of the subhuman Jews. "Representatives of the Reich cannot allow themselves to drink at the poisoned well," he said, hitting his fist on the desk. "A new age has begun, demanding new things from us all. Nothing from the past, except our loyalty, can carry us forward. Adolf Hitler is our only law and our only morality." Otto could hardly believe his ears. He felt as if he were looking at a man who had been possessed by a demon.

Suddenly Waldeck calmed down and began talking about other matters, asking Otto how the staff in New York was working, and what areas needed help, and how the American press could be made to report "a true picture of Germany," and so forth. Then he said goodbye, walked with Otto to the door, and shook his hand.

It was an amazing performance.

The next day Otto had an appointment with Adolf Hitler himself. The Führer was a little taller than he had expected, and quite calm. It was his eyes that caught Otto's attention. They were the eyes of a thief. He didn't just *look* at you when he talked to you, he *watched* you. He asked if it was true that certain Americans were "disturbed" by National Socialism. Otto said that it was true, especially in cities with large Jewish populations, such as New York. Well, Hitler said, most American newspapermen were Jews, so what could one expect? Otto replied that he thought this was not true, although certainly he knew many Jewish reporters in New York. Hitler then gave him a ten-minute lecture on the future of the Third Reich, and stood up. The interview was over. Otto left.

That evening he was invited to a "men's dinner" at the home of the Vice-Chancellor, von Papen, where he talked until the early-morning hours with Hermann Göring, the Nazi Minister President of Prussia. Göring, who had studied Otto's career, told him how proud Germany was of him, and laughed at the articles in Nazi newspapers against him. New, young reporters, eager to serve the party, were just looking for ways to fill up space, he said. Those in Germany who *understood politics* knew how valuable Dr. Otto Kiep was.

So Otto returned to America, and to Hanna, who was expecting their third child, and to a sudden flood of German Jews who came to the consulate for help, not knowing whether they would get help or scorn. On June 2, Hanna had a baby girl, whom they named Hanna Charlotte. She was a beautiful baby, and Otto was delighted.

He found himself, now, in a peculiar position. He had been left at his post. But what *was* his post? In his own mind, he was a representative of the German people. In the mind of the public, he was a representative of Adolf Hitler. How long could he go on? In April and May, hints came to him from the Foreign Office that he needed to be a more vigorous spokesman of the National Socialist spirit. At the end of May, Alfred Rosenberg, Hitler's foreign-policy "expert," denounced him as "politically undependable." The ground was being cut out from under him. And his work load was increasing. He was seeing a dozen Jewish refugees every day, and every day in a hundred ways he had to try to defend Germany without defending National Socialism. On July 14, Hitler issued a law that eliminated all political parties except the National Socialist Party. That was the last straw. On the fifteenth he drafted his resignation, which was formally accepted in Berlin on August 28. A part of his life was over.

American friends began to urge him to stay in the United States, and an article in the magazine *The Nation* did the same:

> The removal of Otto C. Kiep from the German Consulate in New York is one of the hardest blows dealt to the United States by the Hitler Government. . . . Indeed there is every reason to believe that Hitler and his immediate entourage, notably Dr. Rosenberg, his advisor on foreign affairs, are as ignorant of the psychology of other people as were the Kaiser and his aides when war came. As for Dr. Kiep, he had been extremely successful in winning friends for Germany . . . until the coming of Hitler undid it all. The United States would be the gainer if he should decide to remain here permanently.

Otto wished the article hadn't been written, since it could only make his life more difficult, but at the same time he was grateful for it.

He and Hanna began saying goodbye to people and places. He would miss his Manhattan office terribly. It was in the "first building in America," facing Battery Park, with a clear view of the harbor and the Statue of Liberty, a wonderful place to watch ships coming in.

XVI

The New Germany

In October, Hanna Charlotte was baptized in Ballenstedt by Pastor Thieme. (Otto's mother called Thieme "the burying preacher" in honor of his sad, serious manner. She claimed that no one had ever seen him smile.) Tom Watson from New York and his wife and daughter Jane were there, and Jane took on the responsibilities of godmother. Otto went immediately back to Berlin to find a new job. Several possibilities came and went. He was not a party member, and that counted against him. Just after Easter 1934, he was offered the direction of a German trade delegation to South America. He would be given the rank of minister, and the job was "non-political." He took it, and led a very successful mission in spite of a number of difficulties. (The Argentine newspaper *Crítica* called him "a well-known Nazi propagandist," and almost everywhere North American politicians and businessmen tried to block him.)

When he went back to Germany in the spring of 1935 it was like going down in a submarine. The Nazi Party was everywhere—in posters, on the radio (which was now run by the Ministry of Propaganda) , in newspapers, and in conversation. What surprised and depressed Otto was the feeling on the part of so many people that Germany was a much better place now that Hitler was showing the way—that Germany had rediscovered its true character and soul.

In every area of life, people were speaking up enthusiastically in favor of the new vision of the Third Reich. The key word was "co-ordination" (*Gleichschaltung*). Every organization of every kind was required to become a National Socialist organization or be outlawed. Associations of cattle breeders, mathematicians, travel agents, businessmen, all had to "co-ordinate" themselves, pledging allegiance to Adolf Hitler and reorganizing according to the Nazi "leadership principle." Large independent groups were simply wiped out. Not only the political parties but the trade unions were destroyed, carried away by brute force and the Chancellor's decree. Those who saw the Hitler tyranny for what it was, and who wanted to resist, were forced to a terrible "double-facedness," joining Nazi organizations in the hope of defeating the aims of the party, praying and working for Hitler's defeat.

But with the tyranny, good things were happening. More than half of the people who had been out of work in 1933 were working, and more people were getting jobs every day. There was more money in more pockets, and it was sound money. People could think of saving again.

Even Max was becoming interested in National Socialism. He had always loved outdoor activities, and the National Socialists had a feeling for that. It was part of their desire to get back to the soil, back to the roots of the *Germanic experience*. They also had a special concern for youth, for developing healthy bodies through outdoor exercise. Who could be against that?

Otto's mother spoke out against Hitler, but there weren't many who did. (She had recently missed a train because she got involved in lecturing the station agent about *Mein Kampf* and refused to be stopped until she was through.) In one way or another, most Germans seemed to feel the way a grocery-store owner in Ballenstedt felt. "Before Hitler, we had no pride," he said to Otto one day. "Now we look each other in the eye . . . We're proud. We believe in ourselves again. For anything good in this world you have to pay . . . Work is good, pride is good, power is good. A leader to believe in is good . . . So what if I can't buy the newspaper I used to buy? I'll buy another, or listen to the news on the radio, or do something better with my time. And as for getting the Jews out of Germany, I have nothing against that."

On the fourth of March 1935, Otto got a telephone call from Ida. Their father was dying. He left for Ballenstedt immediately. When he got there he found his father in bed in his room. A stroke two years before, when he was eighty-six, had left him partially paralyzed. Now he was so weak his voice had left him. Otto sat down beside him and told him a little of the news from Berlin. Then, slowly, he said what he had said to him before going to war—that he was grateful for his training in work and duty and faithfulness, and that he would continue to multiply the gifts he had been given. His father nodded. His white beard was still perfectly trimmed. Five days later, on March 9, he died.

His father's funeral was an occasion for the gathering of all the Kieps. For Otto it meant getting in touch again with his nieces and nephews, and talking to Max. As a civil servant Max had been under strong pressure to join the National Socialist Party. And he was sympathetic with some of its aims and programs. What did Otto think? It was not a decision, Otto said, that one person could make for another. Some good men had joined, and he might some day have to do it himself, in order to stay in public life. If one believed in the principles of the party, of course, it would be easy. He did not, which made it hard.

He told Max something that had happened to him in South America the year before. Official notice arrived while they were in Santiago, Chile, that they had to take an oath of loyalty to Adolf Hitler. The words of the oath were included with the notice. Once the oath was taken, a copy of it had to be signed by the person taking it and by the person administering it, and the signed oath sent back to Berlin. Those refusing to comply were required to quit the service.

He and his first assistant, Kroll, had both taken the oath, administering it to each other. If they hadn't done it, the second half of the South American mission would have failed. And who would have been hurt? Not Adolf Hitler, but a lot of German workers, not to mention their wives and children. "Adolf Hitler is a disaster for Germany," Otto said. "If he stays in power he will carry us all to ruin. But he *is* in power, and we have to deal with him. An oath is a two-way street. If he betrays us, we won't owe him any allegiance."

At the end of March, Otto and Hanna and the children and the children's nurse, Hertha, went back to Berlin.

Again without a job—the "Einstein case" was still being remembered against him—he was restless and unhappy. He decided it was time to have a large, permanent home in Berlin. He and Hanna found a beautiful house on the Taubertstrasse, near the Grunewald Park, bought it, and hired an architect to make some changes.

During the spring and summer he spent as much time as he could with his children, going for walks, reading books, telling stories, playing games. He invented a character, the "Quick Walker," and told dozens of stories about him, sometimes during walks, sometimes before sending them to bed. He also told stories about a giant named "Gorboduc," who was scary and funny at the same time. Hanna, whom everyone called "Baby," was carried along on every walk and listened carefully to every word of every story, laughing when Albrecht and Hildegard did.

In July he was asked to lead a trade delegation to Japan, China, Manchukuo, and Siam. He spent three months studying the Far East, reading every book he could find and talking to dozens of diplomats and businessmen, and left in October, going by way of the Atlantic Ocean and Canada. Halfway through the trip, Hanna joined him. As in South America, there was a lot of hard bargaining and some strange moments. The man who was to bring him before the Emperor of Manchukuo had once been Chinese military attaché in Berlin, and got him to the palace an hour early so they could drink champagne and talk about "the old days in Berlin" together. As a result, he was drunk and Otto was groggy when they came into the Emperor's presence. Fortunately, the Emperor thought it was funny, and the interview went well.

He and Hanna lived a double life in Asia. There was the life of diplomatic work, with all its social requirements—parties, receptions, tours, and so on, which they enjoyed tremendously—and the life of fear and worry about Germany and the future. Passing from Germany to the world outside was a shock. China and England now seemed more alike than either country seemed like Germany. It was as if demons bearing gifts had secretly possessed their country, and only those who traveled back and forth between Germany and the rest of the world over a period of years could see it. Even in China they met people who had visited Germany since Hitler. Almost all of them praised him. Otto and Hanna felt alone with their fears about the terrible future.

They decided, before they went back, to take Hildegard and Hanna, and maybe Albrecht as well, out of Germany as soon as they could. They had to be saved from being taught in the first and second grade that Hitler was God's greatest gift to the German nation. The easy way was to quit the government and go live in England or the United States. Otto still had job offers in both countries. To get out of Germany without shutting the door on German politics was a much more complicated problem.

When he returned to the Foreign Office in Berlin in 1936 he was introduced to Erich Kordt, a Catholic of strong convictions whose opposition to Hitler was fundamentally *moral*. He saw Nazism for what it was, a religion which demanded a man's soul.

Hoping to undermine the will and blunt the force of National Socialist foreign policy, Kordt had worked his way into the confidence of Joachim von Ribbentrop, one of Hitler's foreign-policy advisors and later his Foreign

Minister. Because of the "Einstein case," there was no chance of recommending Otto for an ordinary embassy post—particularly since his rank was now ambassador. Kordt said he would try to locate another job for him which would put him "on ice" for a while.

In February, with Kordt's help, Otto was sent to London as German representative to the International Commission on Non-Intervention. A civil war was being fought in Spain, and each side was getting outside help. Germany was helping "White Spain," led by General Franco, and Russia was helping "Red Spain." The commission had the job of preventing this foreign aid from reaching either side. It was impossible to do. The commission could, however, through an international police force, limit the aid and make sure that those helping one side didn't start shooting at those helping the other side. Otto's function was to sit with the other commissioners and read reports from agents on the scene. It was hardly a job for a man of his talents, but it would put his two girls in English primary schools, and that meant a lot to him.

Otto went to London in March and began to search for an apartment for his family. It was beautiful being in Hyde Park again and knowing that he would soon be walking through it with Hanna and the children. A month before, he had registered Albrecht in Ilfeld for the Easter term. He admired his son for his quickness and his ability to know what other people were feeling and thinking, but at the same time he worried about his shyness and timidity. How would he behave when he was on his own in the world? Would he be crushed by it? He didn't want to take away Albrecht's ability to feel, but he wished he could give him some more toughness.

He thought that Ilfeld might be the answer. There Albrecht would find a "second family" and at the same time face the orderly competition that would make him stronger. It was certainly worth a try. So, over the objections of Hanna, who thought the school had become far too National Socialist, Albrecht went to Ilfeld after the Easter holiday.

Hanna, it turned out, was absolutely right. Ilfeld had become a school to which leading Nazis sent their sons, and the training there was according to the new vision of the Third Reich. The aim was to produce men absolutely obedient to the Führer. The number-one student—the Primus—was now chosen on the basis of his grades, his devotion to the Nazi cause, his ability to bully the other students, and the party rank of his parents. It was, in every way, the wrong world for Albrecht. When the other students found out that he prayed at night, they crawled into his room on their knees cursing God and pretending to be amazed that He did not strike them dead. Albrecht was usually called "the Englishman," and sometimes "the American." His Bible was stolen, returned, and stolen again six or eight times. He was mocked, he was deserted, and he was laughed at, and behind every joke, every trick, was the face of hate. A classmate said to him at dinner one night, "When I grow up, I'm going to keep three or four people like you for house pets or slaves, just to keep my toilet clean." Everyone thought this was very funny.

The headmaster of the school had to join the party but was not a dedicated Nazi. He was sensible and humane. He was, in fact, a serious Christian. But most of his younger teachers, and some of the old ones, were out to prove that they understood the spirit of the new Germany. What happened in Latin class or Greek class was more or less what had happened in Otto's time, but what went on in the dormitories, where the "strong" were allowed to bully the "weak," and what happened on the semi-military hikes and field exercises, where the boys who couldn't carry thirty pounds on their backs eleven miles through the dark were punished and disgraced, made Ilfeld a small model of the terror state.

None of this came clear for a long time. Albrecht had his pride, and he didn't want to admit defeat. He wanted to prove—to himself and everybody else—that he wasn't weak, so in his letters he tried not to tell what he was really feeling, and at the same time not to lie. He didn't succeed. The tone of his letters was wrong. Otto and Hanna both began to worry about him. When July came they invited one of his teachers, Mr. Ölerich, to come to England with him. There were three reasons for this. It would give Albrecht a special relationship with at least one teacher, it would be a sign of their interest in keeping Albrecht in school, and it would give them a chance to learn about Ilfeld from another point of view.

Mr. Ölerich was very nice, and it was pleasant to tour Scotland with him, but he didn't have much to say, except that he was enjoying his vacation. One evening near the end of vacation Otto and Albrecht left him and went for a walk alone. It was always hard to talk to Albrecht and be sure that you were getting his true feelings. Otto remembered his own childhood and how frightened he had been of his father. He told Albrecht that he knew he wasn't happy at Ilfeld, and that he was willing to take him out if Albrecht wanted to leave. Albrecht said that he didn't want to go back, but that he was willing to go back, and was not afraid. Otto accepted this, and more or less believed it. In any case, he wasn't sending his son back alone, so at the end of August they drove to Newcastle and Otto saw him and Mr. Ölerich off on the steamer *Crasters* for Hamburg.

Otto was back in London on September 1. On the ninth, Louis came over from Hamburg for a few days. He was no longer an ardent Nazi. He had been to a party rally in Nuremberg, and it had frightened him. The thousands of marching men, the flags, the enormous crowd filling the stadium and flooding over into the surrounding fields, the music and singing, the great sigh of pleasure followed by wild cheering when Hitler appeared, had opened his eyes. "Hitler is like a god to these people," he said. "You know it, of course, but until you see it you don't really believe it. It will roll over us all."

A year before, Louis had tried to be appointed Hitler's ambassador to London. Otto had been outraged at him. He was trying not to be any more. Louis was a faithful party member, and Otto despised that, but he was probably going to have to join the party himself before long. One of the few people he knew who hadn't even thought of joining was Klaus. He was going to keep his independence no matter what it cost. And his wife Loria felt the same. But Klaus was not trying to stay in political life. The only thing that bothered Otto now was Louis's willingness to "run with the hounds," to choose whichever side was winning and pretend to be a true believer. Otto took out a clipping from the London *Daily Express* and handed it to Louis. It was an article by former Prime Minister Lloyd George, calling Hitler "the George Washington of Germany." Louis read it. "Well," he said, "you have to admit that the man has done some amazing things."

And Otto had to admit that his brother was right. Hitler had done some amazing things.

Once his work was organized, Otto had more time to himself than he had had since he was young. He began to read the New Testament again, keeping a copy on the table next to his bed. He had always been loyal to the church, celebrating its holidays, enjoying the company of devout men like Emmanuel Winkler, and praying the church's prayer of thanksgiving with real feeling, but sin and salvation, the struggle between darkness and light, had always seemed to him to be outdated.

Now the New Testament way of looking at the world suddenly made sense. That great evil could appear with gifts for everyone—jobs, order, a sense of purpose, religious enthusiasm—and mask its hatred with noble-sounding slogans was something Jesus had understood and talked about, and Adolf Hitler was now revealing. Hitler had always insisted that National Socialism was not a party but a movement, a "national rising." A party seeks political power, he said, while a movement seeks to change men by possessing them. A party has politicians and a program, a movement has a leader and his vision. Hitler put himself before the German people as *Savior,* demanding faith and obedience. More and more every day Otto saw his choice as between Hitler and Christ.

Every week a letter came from Albrecht full of good cheer and news, but with strain and fear underneath.

When he came home for the Christmas holidays, it was clear that he should not be sent back. The school was breaking his spirit. Otto wrote the headmaster and told him that Albrecht would not complete the term in January.

He worried about how the headmaster might reply. If he blamed Albrecht for dropping out, it could damage the rest of his school career in Germany. Fortunately, the headmaster understood clearly what was at stake. He took the blame for Albrecht's leaving on himself.

31 Dec. 1937

Dear Dr. Kiep:

I am acknowledging your son's withdrawal from school.

Personally I regret very much that your decision to send Albrecht to Ilfeld resulted in this failure. I am somewhat concerned that this result is in part due to the fact that our education is too standardized and leaves little room for more individualized educational care.

Please greet Albrecht for me. I wish you and your family a Happy New Year. Thank you for your regards to my wife and me.

Heil Hitler

Dr. von Drygalski

The year 1938 began, then, with all three children in English schools and the family in 2, Rutland Cottages, south of Hyde Park. The apartment was a little small, but the family was together.

XVII

Before the Storm

On the night of November 9, 1938, squads of Nazis in every major German city broke into stores and offices and homes belonging to Jews. Property was burned, smashed, and stolen, and those who tried to interfere were beaten. This outburst of hatred was celebrated in the Nazi press as an expression of the way all patriotic Germans felt about "those bacteria still infecting the national bloodstream."

To Otto, "Crystal Night" was a sure signal that war was coming. Hitler was ready to defy the world. He had been encouraged in his defiance by the British Prime Minister, Neville Chamberlain, and Chamberlain's ambassador in Berlin, Nevile Henderson, who admired Hitler tremendously and was anxious that Britain cooperate with him. Henderson was absolutely sure that, in his heart, Hitler loved peace.

Two months before, Chamberlain had flown to Munich to meet with Hitler. The whole Kiep clan was in Ballenstedt at the time to celebrate Mrs. Kiep's eightieth birthday. The day after Chamberlain arrived, a German-English Non-Aggression Declaration was announced.

When the news came over the radio there was rejoicing in the Kiep house. But Otto did not rejoice. Hitler had demanded a bargain with Britain, and gotten it. He would be more sure than ever that the English had become "womanish," and that he could do what he liked. The balance of power in Europe had shifted in Germany's favor. Otto's mother, hearing the news, made a face as if she were going to spit. "Chamberlain is an old woman," she said.

Two days after that, Otto drove with Hanna to Wedderstedt for a dinner party at Ida's. He had been there in May for the funeral of Ida's son Christoph, who had died suddenly of blood poisoning. The household was still living under the shadow of that event, but Otto's coming was always reason to celebrate, so the party was lively. Ida's three girls were now young women, and Otto enjoyed performing for them.

Toward the end of the meal they began to talk about politics, which for Otto meant talking about the coming war. Within two years, he said, German troops would strike at the west. France, Denmark, Sweden, and Norway would be attacked. After that, foreign bombers would come and destroy all the cities of Germany. "Then we will be lucky if we still have a roof over our heads."

Two guests, Mr. and Mrs. Schafer, got up before he was through and asked for their coats. They were outraged by what he had said. Now was a time for faith in Germany and Germany's Leader, not a time for fear and distrust. After they left, Ida came back to the table very upset, not because of the Schafers but because of Otto's lack of caution. She lectured him about speaking out.

"Ida," he said, "the whole world is lying. Someone must tell the truth."

For Christmas 1938, Otto and Hanna decided to take the children to the winter resort Arosa in Switzerland for two weeks. Just before they left, Otto was invited by the Foreign Office to come to the Wilhelmstrasse to discuss a new assignment. Hanna and the children went ahead to Arosa, and Otto went to Berlin. When his business was over, he would meet them at the resort.

In Berlin he was treated with great courtesy. People who had been cool to him a few years before now acted quite friendly. It had been decided in the highest councils of National Socialism that certain Germans who had emigrated to foreign countries should be called back to their Fatherland. The Führer was seeking skilled workers between the ages of twenty and forty-five, and the more children they had, the better. Would Otto, with his long experience in the United States and his numerous contacts in the American press, be interested in heading a "reparations bureau" in New York or some other suitable city? He would be able to offer each "racially pure" German family free transportation home, generous assistance in finding suitable housing, and the guarantee of a job to fit the worker's skill.

The moment the offer was made, Otto knew that he would have to turn it down. He would not try to lure men and their families into *this* Germany. He was not, however, going to say that right away. Instead, he inquired seriously about all the details of the plan, raised possible problems, and in every way acted like a candidate for the job. He was amazed at how sure the top officials at the Foreign Office were that the United States was full of Germans desperately eager to come home, and only waiting for the proper approach. They refused to see that Germany was becoming, in the eyes of the world, a criminal nation, and that trying to get large numbers of Germans to come back was a fool's errand. German-Americans meeting each other on East Eighty-sixth Street in Manhattan might talk about what a great man Hitler was, but praising the new Germany was a long way from getting on a boat and going there.

Most of the people Otto knew at the Foreign Office were not as hopeful as the men at the top were. They knew what Germany had become, and they were afraid. But they felt powerless to raise doubts. What good would it do? So the game of pretending to believe in Hitler went on.

At the end of the week Otto turned down the job and submitted a report on the difficulty of getting people in other countries to return to Germany at present.

He brought his family back to London in the middle of January. The work of the Commission on Non-Intervention was coming to an end. It had been dull work, but that was because the agents operating in Spain had been so efficient. For the first time a many-nation military organization had been put together to prevent the spread of war. It was the kind of work the League of Nations should have been doing from the beginning, and never did.

All during his London stay Otto had kept pretty much away from the German embassy, which was a mixed garden of old friends, new Nazis, and unknowns. Instead,

he had associated almost entirely with English friends—
old Mrs. Bower and her daughter Maudie, a Quaker who
was helping Jewish refugees; Barclay Baron, with whom
he had once listened to law lectures at the University of
Munich; Colonel James, at whose estate they spent many
weekends walking and horseback riding.

In the spring of 1939, after the German attack on
Czechoslovakia, he deepened his contact with the one
man at the embassy whom he trusted absolutely, Theo
Kordt, Erich Kordt's brother. They talked again and
again about the coming war. Should they stay in England
and sit it out, or go back? Otto thought the war would
begin in late 1939 or early 1940 and last four years: two
years for German victories, two years for German defeats.
During that time, the power of the army would grow and
the power of the National Socialist politicians would
diminish. The thing to do, if they returned to Germany,
was to enter the army. And there was really no question
of returning or not returning. They would both go back.
Hitler would have to be overthrown, and that couldn't be
done by Germans living in London. And if Germany was
going to suffer, the only way to serve her would be to live
through her sufferings with her.

It was impossible to tell the future, but one thing was
clear: the British and French, by letting Hitler have his
way, had made him much stronger and harder to elimi-
nate. They had confirmed him in the minds of the Nazi
faithful, and in his own mind, as a military and political
genius. How was Hitler to be brought down when he
controlled everything the German people saw and heard,
when he had an enormous secret police force, and when
everything he promised came true?

XVIII

Resisting

OTTO and Hanna were not going to stop living because war was coming. They knew a young Englishwoman, Ruth Lush, whom they wanted to bring to Germany with them for a year. She would be able to improve her German and help keep up the children's English. They discussed the idea with her and promised that if anything happened they would get her back to England. She wanted to go with them, and so it was arranged. The family went in stages back to Berlin, and by the first week in August, everyone was there.

Otto and Hanna set about creating an order of life for the time to come. Like Eskimos getting ready for the long polar night, they laid in supplies, saw to the care of their children—Albrecht went to boarding school at Templin, which, unlike Ilfeld, was not a party training school, while Hildegard and Baby were registered in the Grunewald school where Illi Grisson taught—and fell back on the family and a small circle of friends. Otto made a special effort to get on even closer terms with Hanna's father, and succeeded.

In a very systematic way he wrote letters to friends in

other countries—first in England, then in the United States. (One letter went to Oskar Weigert, who had fled Germany and was now living in Washington.) Each letter was different and personal, and most of them were in Hanna's name as well as his own. He tried not to let them sound like farewell letters. They were not meant to be. They were official announcements that the Kieps had changed their address again, and could now be written to and visited at Taubertstrasse 15, Berlin-Grunewald, Germany. But because Otto knew that the iron doors were about to slam shut, they felt to him like farewell letters, and probably sounded that way to those who received them.

As the circle of friends grew smaller and more private, they discovered the friendship of conspirators. Most of the people they knew well despised Hitler, but not all of them were willing to hear him criticized, or to discuss Germany's dangerous future. The truth was too painful for them. When Otto spoke to them about politics and the future, they changed the subject. "Please," they seemed to be saying, "we don't want to know the truth. It's too painful." Other friends were willing to risk talking and preparing themselves for the future. One such man was Helmuth von Moltke. Moltke was a good deal younger than Otto, but they had a lot in common. They both had studied law in England as well as Germany, they were both German patriots who nevertheless loved England, they were both interested in international law, and they both rejected National Socialism on moral and religious as well as political grounds.

Moltke was an idealist, Protestant in religion and socialist in politics. He wanted to prepare himself and those who shared his outlook for the time after Hitler. He was convinced that Hitler and Germany would have to suffer complete defeat before a new beginning would be possible. But after that defeat, how was the new government to be chosen? How was it to be organized? How was individual freedom to be guaranteed? Moltke was especially interested in the crucial first months after the war. So much depended upon how the new beginning was made.

A circle of people had gathered around him and his wife, meeting both in their Berlin apartment and at Kreisau, his family estate in Silesia. Otto was never at the heart of the Kreisau Circle—his own experience and training made him more politically conservative than Moltke—but they became good friends. One member of the circle, Adam von Trott zu Solz, he found particularly interesting and attractive. He, too, had studied in England and traveled in America and Asia in the service of the Foreign Office, and he, too, saw National Socialism as a moral and spiritual disease.

In August, with the children safe at home with Ruth Lush and Ida's two younger daughters, Elizabeth and Irmgard, who were in Berlin for a holiday, Otto and Hanna decided to take a short vacation. They drove east by way of Dresden to Prague, which was now occupied by German troops, and then started back, planning to visit Kreisau on the way.

Near Kreisau the roads suddenly filled up with army trucks moving east toward the Polish border. War was very close, perhaps only two or three days away. They turned west and drove straight through to Berlin, arriving early on the morning of August 26. As they passed through the suburbs, they saw trenches being dug for antiaircraft guns.

Ruth was awakened and told to pack her things as quickly as possible. There was a train for Rotterdam at noon, with good connections with a ship for home. Elizabeth and Irmgard got up and were told to pack too, and Otto called Ida to tell her when they would get to Wedderstedt. Ida had been waiting for his call. Walter, who was a member of the army reserve, had already received a notice to report for duty.

By dinnertime, all three of the visitors were gone.

Hitler had a special hatred for the Poles and had promised to deal ruthlessly with them "in the event of war." Otto wondered if he should tell Hanna what could be expected in Poland after the German victory. Certainly it would upset her, but nevertheless he decided that he should. There might come a time when he would have to keep things from her for her safety. Otherwise, he owed it to her to be at least as honest with her as he was with anyone. So that night, after the two girls were in bed, they discussed what this war would mean to the Poles, and especially the Polish Jews. "It will be a nightmare," he said. "The shame of it will be remembered for a thousand years."

Hitler attacked Poland two days later. On September 3, Britain and France declared war. That afternoon, Illi Grisson came for tea. She and Otto and Hanna sat on the terrace behind the house and talked about Hildegard's schoolwork and the war. Illi had a surprising interest in military matters, and Otto answered her questions as well as he could. When, she asked, would the outcome of the war be decided? Did Otto think there would be one decisive battle?

"Illi, my child," Otto said—Illi was then forty-seven years old—"the decisive battle of the war was fought today, in England. When the English declared war on us, the war was lost. In the next months, we will win amazing victories. The German army is a great army. But all that we win we will have to lose, and the cost will be terrible. Find a reliable bomb shelter. I am absolutely serious about that. If they assign you a poor one, let me know."

On September 17, Soviet troops crossed the Polish border from the east, and in a few more days German and Russian troops had occupied the entire Polish state. This "elimination of the Polish menace" had been agreed upon by Hitler and Stalin as part of a German-Soviet Non-Aggression Pact a week before the Polish campaign. The campaign was reported in the German newspapers and over the state radio as "a glorious victory in every respect."

Before the fighting was over in Poland, with the help of his friend Hans Oster, Otto was given "active" status in the army and assigned to the military High Command, the Oberkommando der Wehrmacht (O.K.W.) in the Office of Counter-Intelligence, which was headed by Admiral Wilhelm Canaris. Both Canaris and Oster were active anti-Hitler men. Otto's task was to keep track of the foreign press so that the High Command would know the state of public feeling in enemy countries. It became his duty to begin each day by reading the London *Times,* something he had done every morning for years. He also read other foreign newspapers, listened to certain foreign broadcasts, and read summaries of other broadcasts from army sources. He became one of the few men in Germany with a clear, balanced view of world events.

Early in December, Otto's mother suddenly fell sick. For a few days she said she didn't need a doctor. When one was finally called, she asked him if he was a National Socialist. He said he was. She turned her face to the wall and refused to let him examine her. He guessed at her illness from her looks and the symptoms that were reported to him, and prescribed medicine, but it was too late. Perhaps even the best doctor in the world couldn't have helped her. She grew weaker every day. The sons were called home, and Ida came over from Wedderstedt.

She didn't want to die, she told Ida, because she wanted "to find out what is going to happen to that criminal." She was worried, too, about Otto. "Politics will finally kill him," she said. "You must do everything you can for him."

On December 19, she died. On the evening before the funeral, with all the Kiep families gathered together, Otto made a short speech. "With this event," he said, "our family has lost its center, a gap has suddenly occurred which cannot be filled. Up until the end, Charlotte Kiep was to her children what she had been in their youth, an incomparable mother who devoted her life to her children, an important and wise woman and indomitable worker, and a German filled with passionate patriotism. She gave her children, in addition to healthy bodies and other natural gifts, the best education that a mother can give. She gave us ideals, and she led for us a life of the highest possible example. Her life will not be forgotten, and her grave will be honored by us all."

In January, Otto recommended Helmuth von Moltke for a post in the legal department of the O.K.W., and he was taken on. His presence increased the spirit of resistance and humanity in the Canaris/Oster group, which at the time was the most effective branch of the anti-Hitler resistance. Both Canaris and Oster were working to undermine the National Socialist terror. Oster, in April of 1940, took it upon himself to warn the Dutch of the date of the German invasion, in the hope of reducing, at least, the scope of the German victory. His warning had no effect. Holland was attacked on May 10 and surrendered, after the near destruction of Rotterdam by bombs, on May 15. Canaris, a very private man, was constantly risking himself to save men and women from the hands of the secret police.

Otto settled into a certain work routine, and life in the house at Taubertstrasse 15 went on in an orderly and peaceful way. The family went to the opera and to concerts a little more often than they had in England, partly because the girls were getting old enough really to enjoy music and partly as a relief from the strain of work and worry.

On June 2, Baby was seven years old. There was a wonderful birthday party, and because she liked it so much, Otto put on his army uniform for the occasion. He wore his uniform as little as possible. Even at the O.K.W., he usually worked in civilian clothes. He had been proud of his uniform in the 1914–18 war. Now he felt almost ashamed to be seen in it with its Nazi symbols.

On June 14, after a campaign that had lasted only five weeks, Paris surrendered to German troops. France had fallen. Soon after, heavy German air raids began on England. The rumor in Berlin was that England would be invaded in the spring of 1941. The tempo of the war left everyone breathless, and Hitler was seen more and more as a genius or a god. He had been in power for seven years, and never been defeated.

More and more, Otto felt the obligation to tell people what could be expected in the future. The only information that most of his friends had came from the state newspapers and radio and from rumor. By means of his work at the O.K.W., Otto could see Germany from the outside, and put Hitler's victories in perspective. Often enough when he spoke there were strangers in the room— strangers who might be Gestapo spies. Again and again Hanna, his brothers, Ida, his friends, even people he didn't know very well, begged him to be more careful, but he couldn't. He *had* to tell what he knew. "We are surrounded by lies. People must know that there are still Germans who love the truth."

As the months passed, he came more and more to feel that the truth was both his vocation and his weapon of resistance. Often enough, as a diplomat and a lawyer, it had been his job to emphasize certain facts and ignore others, to balance one version of the truth with another, to call attention to the laws that would help his case. Now, in a world committed to lies, he could not join the liars.

Oster and others depended upon him for certain "official" resistance work—to carry particular news to particular people, warn this man or that of a surprise inspection to come, sign a paper which would assist in freeing someone from suspicion, and so on—but nothing he did was more important than being an honest and well-informed man in the midst of liars.

He knew, of course, that those who warned him against speaking were perfectly right in what they said—the Gestapo *was* everywhere, and once a man fell into its hands, almost nothing could be done for him. To be arrested by the Gestapo was to be condemned. Every day people simply disappeared, and were never seen alive again. Still, he went on speaking.

In December 1941, the United States entered the war.

Irmgard Westphal was now doing her "practical year" at the Kaiser Wilhelm Institute for Plant Research in Müncheberg, not far from Berlin. This meant she could visit almost every weekend. Otto had a special feeling for Irmgard because she was Ida's youngest and because Hildegard and Baby liked her so much. She was a very independent girl, but not at all snobbish or self-important. She became part of the Sunday afternoon tea circle on the terrace, and listened in on the conversation and sometimes spoke up.

One Sunday Helmuth von Moltke and his wife were there, and Moltke was describing what he had seen during a recent trip through Belgium, Holland, and France—the unbelievably hard conditions under which the conquered people were forced to live.

"Isn't it terrible?" Irmgard said. "Here we are, sitting in peace and quiet sipping tea, knowing about what's happening in the outside world, and still just staying safe."

Von Moltke smiled at her. "Don't push, young lady, we will all get our turn."

The war began to go against Germany at the beginning of 1943. In February, the German army around Stalingrad was surrounded and destroyed in a long and cruel battle. The German General Staff had long felt betrayed by Hitler. Now for the first time the soldier in the line—and his family at home—felt betrayed.

One of General Oster's sons was a victim of Stalingrad. Ordered to lead his men in a senseless attack, he had chosen to die alone instead. The General and his wife came over to Otto's house the day they received the news. Oster was speechless with grief and outrage. It was too much for him to bear.

On March 13 a bomb was put on board Hitler's plane returning from staff meetings behind the Eastern Front. Otto knew about it from Oster, and expected a phone call late in the afternoon telling him that Hitler's plane had gone down. The phone call never came. The bomb failed to explode. His job, if the bomb had gone off, would have been to serve as Press Chief for the new government. There was no question in his mind that the Allies would fall on Germany with their whole weight in the case of Hitler's death and a German surrender. Germany would have about three weeks between the *coup d'état* and occupation by foreign troops. In those three weeks Germany's case before the world would have to be made, and no one was as well suited to make that case as he, or as likely to be believed.

He was divided in his own mind about the wisdom of killing Hitler, but once he knew that the bomb was going on the plane, he was bitterly disappointed that it didn't go off. Disappointed, and exhausted by the tension. As in 1924–25, only in a far worse way, he was plagued by sleeplessness. He would get up at one or two in the morning, walk the floor, try to read, get an apple out of the basement, and go over in his mind the same questions again and again. Sometimes Hanna would wake up and come into his study with a look of the most terrible distress on her face. He *had* to try to sleep, she would tell him.

"How can I sleep," he would say, "when I am in pain over my country?"

The summer of 1943 passed, part of it spent in Berlin and part in Wedderstedt, where there was more food. Ida made a special effort to feed Otto. "You're going to make me fat, Ida," he warned her. Berlin was getting more and heavier air raids all the time, and he and Hanna made arrangements to have the girls come to the farm in the fall. While he was in Wedderstedt, Ida asked him please to talk to Irmgard. She was letting more and more people know how she felt about National Socialism. She had stopped saying "Heil Hitler" when meeting people, even government workers and strong Nazis. She was telling "defeatist" jokes to her friends. She would surely be arrested. "I've already lost my son and my husband," Ida said—Walter had been killed in an automobile accident in February 1940. "It would be too much if Irmgard went too."

Otto went to her room to see her, and told her what her mother had said to him. "I think you're being very foolish," he said. "This is a time to take care." Irmgard was shocked that *he* should tell her to be careful.

"You say things against them all the time," she said.

"Dear child," he said, "my profession is politics, I must speak. If I were silent now, I would have no right to speak later. But you have no such obligation."

"Didn't you say that a person had to speak the truth?" she asked.

"It is a question of your conscience, I know that," he said, "but be aware of what is at stake. No joke against Hitler, no refusal to give the salute, is worth your life."

He didn't want to discuss his own conscience, which was in this case not important. He wanted to convince her to be more cautious. She was too young to be hurt for nothing. She still seemed angry and puzzled.

"As it is, Irmgard," he said, "when this is over, people will say to me, 'If you were against them, why weren't you in a concentration camp? Why are you still alive? How did you escape, unless you too were a Nazi?' "

"No one will ever say that to you, Uncle Otto," she said. "I won't let them."

The beginnings of defeat made the Nazis even more desperate to crush their enemies inside Germany. In the summer of 1943 General Oster was taken out of the O.K.W. and put on reserve. They suspected him of belonging to the resistance, but had no proof. The next step was arrest. In order to avoid being arrested at night, which was when the Gestapo preferred to take people, he and his wife began sleeping in the children's wing of the Kiep house, arriving some time after dinner and leaving before breakfast. Albrecht was away for a year with a "work service" battalion of the Hitler Youth and the girls were in Wedderstedt, so that part of the house was free.

On the ninth of September, Italy surrendered to the Allies. The country which had been bound to Germany by a "pact of steel" was no longer on her side. The next day Otto went to a tea party in the small apartment of Elisabeth von Thadden on the Kramerstrasse. He had planned to be in Wedderstedt that day, but a bombing raid two nights before had broken windows and cracked walls at the house, and he was staying to look after repairs. He was disappointed not to go to Wedderstedt, where Hanna and the girls were, and the tea was something of a "duty," though he admired Elisabeth von Thadden very much. She had come to Berlin in 1941 after the school she directed—the Wieblingen School, near Heidelberg—had been closed by the Reich Ministry of Education. Unlike the people at Ilfeld, she had not been ready to make "National Socialist reforms."

At the tea party were former Staatsekretär Zarden and his daughter Irmgard; Dr. Hilger van Scherpenberg, a legation secretary in the Foreign Office; an old friend of Elisabeth's, Fanny von Kurowski; Mrs. Solf, the widow of the former ambassador to Japan; and a young physician whom Otto had never met before, Dr. Reckzeh.

The talk was largely about the Italian surrender. Otto was surprised to find people talking as if it made some difference in the final outcome of the war. Dr. Reckzeh, especially, was interested in discussing whether Germany's "prospects" had changed. What did Major Kiep think?

"After this, only a miracle can save Germany," he said. "That is quite clear."

After a while the talk turned to the bombing of Berlin, and how bad it was likely to become. "Berlin is necessarily the one great target," Otto said. "That it is the capital is enough to make it so." He mentioned Hanna's sister Lu, who was expecting a baby and whom he had already urged to leave the city. He took out an aerial photograph, which had been printed in *The New York Times,* showing the pattern of British and American bombing in the city. It was quite clear, he said, that the aim was to destroy as many homes as possible, to terrorize the whole population of the city. The photograph was passed around the circle.

Shortly before Otto left, Dr. Reckzeh offered to serve as a courier for anyone who wanted to send messages to friends in Switzerland. He had already agreed to take a message for Miss von Thadden. He knew, he said, a certain Pastor Müller, who was operating a communications center near Lucerne. Several of those around the table promised letters, but Otto shook his head and said that he had only one friend there, the brother-in-law of former Economics Minister Neuhaus, a Mr. Finkler. Dr. Reckzeh then offered to deliver Otto's calling card to him as a gesture of courtesy. Otto gave him the card, first writing Finkler's address on it. "Greet him for me, if it's convenient," he said. A few minutes later he left.

Lucerne was, in fact, a small "communications center" for Otto, too. He went there once a year to visit Finkler and send and receive mail. Through that mailbox he had learned in November of 1941 that Ruth Lush was married, and in November 1942 that she was expecting a baby.

One morning during the third week in September, Helmuth von Moltke came to Otto's office with a copy of Dr. Reckzeh's report about the tea. He was a Gestapo spy. He had reported the whole event in great detail, and singled out Otto's remarks as especially "defeatist." Defeatism was high treason, punishable by death. It was certain that Otto and the others at the tea would sooner or later be arrested. The Gestapo didn't have to hurry.

Otto had an appointment with Elisabeth von Thadden the next day for lunch at the Cavalry Club. When they met he told her about Reckzeh, and gave an account of his report. He had drawn up two lists, a list of things which could be admitted and a list of things which would have to be denied. It could be admitted, for example, that they had discussed the terror raids against Berlin, and that he had shown everyone the *Times* photograph, which in the meantime had been reprinted in the party newspaper as an example of the blood-thirst of the enemy. About Otto's "defeatist" remarks, they agreed to say that they were of a *detached* and *objective* kind, like a lecture to army officers or officials at the Foreign Office. He had been speaking in a "professional" way. After discussing their story, and deciding how to contact the others, he assured her that this was bound to have happened sooner or later, and that he saw a chance, now that they had been warned and could agree about their story, to escape with only prison sentences. "And you and I are the ones they want. The others may get away free."

He told Hanna that night. It was common for the wives of "political criminals" to be arrested along with their husbands. It was a way of warning every traitor that he was inviting punishment not only upon himself but also upon his wife. Sometimes teenage children were arrested, too. Hanna took the news calmly, but he could see that it shocked her and frightened her. She didn't cry in front of him, but he knew she would surely cry alone in her room that night, and not out of fear for herself.

Up until now he had always told her whatever he knew about the plans and activities of the resistance. The people belonging to it were not just *his* friends but *their* friends. Hanna was acquainted with Canaris and knew Oster well. Earlier in the war, Oster had come by every Sunday morning on his horse—riding was his favorite exercise—and she would send Hildegard to the front gate with a goblet of beer for him to drink, which he always finished in one long pull. She knew of the importance of Carl Goerdeler, the former Lord Mayor of Leipzig, and of General Ludwig Beck, who would direct the next attempt to kill Hitler. She knew, in fact, too much.

He would tell her no more.

The less she knew, the easier it would be for her to play the innocent and simple wife. They went over the names of all the people about whom the Gestapo might ask. It would be safe to admit knowing almost all of them, but only "in a social way." In the event of her arrest she would have to trust herself, and he would have to trust her, to say what was convincing and politically safe. He had no doubt that she would be able to do it. The skills she had used to charm senators in the garden of the house on Idaho Avenue would not desert her in conversations with the Gestapo.

They had Christmas with the family in Wedderstedt. There was a pageant on Christmas Eve at the village church, and then everyone walked home through the snow. When they got there they put on evening clothes, sang carols around the Christmas tree, and opened presents. It was beautiful.

He had already told Ida in September, when they were together to remember their mother's birthday, that he expected to be arrested. Since then she had read again all his letters to her, and burned those with anti-Hitler references. Not many letters were left. He told her now that he expected arrest before the end of January, and that she would be visited by the Gestapo. He had clothing, some old papers, and other personal belongings in the room she kept for him. "You can let them search without worrying," he said. "There's nothing here that could hurt me."

The last thing was to tell Albrecht, who was going into the navy in the spring. Otto did it as soon as he got back to Berlin. There was no way to make it easy for him, so he told him directly and clearly the entire story of his betrayal by Reckzeh. "I could be arrested at any time," he said, "and I think it will not be long now." Ignoring Albrecht's disbelief, he then spoke about the war. It was hard enough, he said, for a man to risk his life in a just cause. To do it in an unjust cause was almost too much for the spirit to bear. That is what every German was doing, whether he was in uniform or not. The best a man in Albrecht's position could do was to dedicate himself to protecting his comrades.

Albrecht wanted to know what would happen to Otto after he was arrested. "I will be sent to a prison or concentration camp, and then put on trial, probably at the People's Court, though possibly before a military court, and after that, who can say? By then, Albrecht, you are very likely to be at sea."

"I'll get a leave to be with you if that happens," Albrecht said.

Otto put his hand on his son's arm. "Whatever happens to me, I want you to know that it is because I tried to speak the truth out of love for Germany. We are in the same war, Albrecht, only in different places. If one of us is disgraced, or falls, the other must not be discouraged, or fail in his duty to his comrades."

Albrecht didn't answer, but he understood.

XIX

The Bridge of Love

On Sunday, January 16, a little before four in the morning, three S.S. men came in a car to arrest Otto. It helped to have Albrecht there. It gave him a reason to be calm. He put on his uniform, gave Albrecht some instructions about repairing some bomb damage on the house, and said goodbye.

At the S.S. headquarters a man read him his discharge from the army. He was shown the paper, asked to sign a statement that it had been read to him in full, and ordered to remove his uniform. He was now beyond the reach of military courts, where he might have received a fair and orderly trial.

After a few days he was taken to the concentration camp at Ravensbrück, near Fürstenburg, and given a cell below ground. There was a cot with a straw sack and a blanket, a table and chair, and a toilet. High up in one wall was a small window. The building was made of stone, cold and damp.

He set about to order his life as much as he could. There were certain things that gave him strength and hope. The first of these things was Hanna's love, on which he could depend absolutely. It was *his,* regardless of how far away she was or what came between them. Not everyone in his family liked her, and he had been blamed, even by his mother, for needing her too much, and making too much of her. No matter. She was the one great fact of his life, and he drew strength from their passion.

He could depend, too, on Ida's care of the children if Hanna was arrested, and on Hanna's father doing everything possible to help him. There was not much that anyone could do, but he had contacts with all kinds of people. He would not soon run out of things to try.

All his life Otto had done what he could to keep his own soul, not to betray himself or his country. He had worked to remain a man no matter what others might do. Now his fate had been taken out of his hands. He had never liked to say "God will provide," or "God will show the way," but now God would have to provide, and he tried to put himself completely in God's hands.

He was questioned and questioned again, sometimes two or three times in one day. Always behind the questioning was the threat of torture if he didn't admit what they wanted him to admit, that he had been in contact with former Chancellor Wirth, now living in Switzerland, and that he and Wirth and other enemies of the Third Reich were working for the defeat of Germany in hopes of getting power for themselves.

Who was conspiring with him?

What were Wirth's plans?

What part would Otto play in the new government?

With whom was he in correspondence in the enemy countries?

These questions were asked in a hundred different ways, over and over again, in every tone of voice. He was questioned until he was sick with fatigue. Then, for no clear reason, the questioning would stop, sometimes with thanks, sometimes with threats.

He tried not to let his nerves be worn down, or to let his body get out of condition. For years he had done exercises every day—lifting weights which had once belonged to his father and going for a morning run. He continued to begin every morning with fifteen or twenty minutes of exercises. And he made himself eat all the food he was given, regardless of how bad it was.

He was not allowed to write to anyone about his case or about his treatment in Ravensbrück. He could write only personal letters to members of his family. He had always planned out every letter before writing it. Now, for the mental exercise, he made more careful preparations than ever, planning his letters to Hanna in his mind, working on the best way to say what he wanted to say before starting to write.

Not long before Christmas they had read aloud Thornton Wilder's novel, *The Bridge of San Luis Rey*. At the end of that novel a woman thinks about memory and death:

> . . . soon we shall die and . . . be loved for a while and forgotten. But the love will have been enough; all those impulses of love return to the love that made them. Even memory is not necessary for love. There is a land of the living and a land of the dead and the bridge is love, the only survival, the only meaning.

To recall those words to her, he wrote a poem, "The Bridge of Love." Writing it brought him out of prison for a few hours, gave him a victory to share with her, helped him to stay mentally alive and flexible.

Hanna, too, was a prisoner in Ravensbrück, as he learned from hints in her letters. She was behaving as he knew she would behave, with every appearance of innocence. For the Gestapo she knew only that her husband was absolutely loyal and faithful to her and Germany. When threats were made against her children, she pretended not to believe them. Her children were loyal and faithful to their parents and to the Hitler Youth. She refused to believe that the party they trusted would turn upon them and betray them. Her questioners had a hard time dealing with her. She looked like the party's ideal German woman, tall, with long blond hair falling below her waist, tied to husband and children and nation and home, intelligent and somewhat fierce, like a Germanic huntress.

One day in late February he saw her. He was being taken to be questioned, and she was moving in the other direction with a Gestapo guard. Suddenly he saw her coming through the doorway. For a moment or two they looked at each other. If their guards had seen any sign of recognition between them, one of them would immediately have been sent to another prison. They gave no sign except in their eyes, but for both of them it was a shock and a priceless gift. That night Otto wrote her a poem:"I saw you. It was a dream, / Yet so clear, it was like reality . . ."

The constant questioning made one thing clear to him. He was going to be executed. He started to write a memoir of his life for his children, so that they would know clearly the heritage they had from their parents. He wrote every chance he got, and he was amazed at how much and how clearly he remembered. And remembering somehow helped him to keep strong.

The knowledge that he was doomed also led him to consider suicide. He had always tried to run his life in a reasonable way—not coldly but wisely, not just serving his own desires and wishes, but at the same time taking good care of himself. Now he was faced with a fact, and he had to calm his mind and think clearly about it. A public trial at the People's Court would find him guilty of treason. When the verdict was passed, all his property would be taken by the state. Hanna and the children would be left without an inheritance, at least until the defeat of Hitler, and perhaps much longer.

Moreover, at any time he might be tortured for information about others who were "defeatist" or had spoken or acted against the government. He would not be able to be silent forever. He was human. He could be broken. Then he would sign whatever they wanted him to sign, and others would be dragged down with him.

It was sensible, then, for him to kill himself. He must prepare Hanna by making his reasons clear to her, letting her know that it was not the suicide of despair but of reason. And he must prepare himself by keeping a clear head, staying as healthy as possible, and gathering the materials of his death, a razor and sleeping pills. He would not, in any case, kill himself at Ravensbrück. Hanna was too close.

Two or three days a week the prisoners in his section were taken out one by one for exercise. Watched by a guard, they walked back and forth in an L-shaped yard. One day in late February he glanced up when he came to the corner of the L and saw Hanna's face in a third-story window. He raised his hand a little to signal that he had seen her. It was almost the end of the exercise period, and after seeing her twice more, he was led back inside. The next time he went out he looked up right away. She had made cards with letters on them, and held them up one by one as he walked, spelling out the word B R I D G E. For the rest of the time she watched him.

She was a wonder.

One Sunday afternoon, to his complete surprise, he was given an hour alone with her. The S.S. guards were never there on weekends, and the camp was in charge of "cal-factors." One of them, who knew that Otto would be transferred to another prison the next day, opened his cell and with hardly a word led him to hers and left them alone for an hour. It was a beautiful meeting, and a terrible parting.

As he stood in the yard the next day waiting to be taken to the gate, he had one more chance to see her. She spelled out for him the first words of Faust's meditation on Easter, "From ice set free . . ." He recited the whole meditation to himself, knowing that she was doing the same thing, and it brought them back together again.

He was taken to the prison in Brandenburg so that he would be nearer Berlin. His trial had been scheduled for July 1. The warden, Herbert Thümmler, tried to treat Otto like a human being, letting him send out and receive mail without opening it, allowing him to receive as many packages as he wanted, and giving him news of his friends. Through Thümmler he learned of the arrest of Helmuth von Moltke, who was also charged with treason. Through him, too, he sent out the memoir for his children.

He had collected enough sleeping pills. This was obviously the place and time to carry out the decision to kill himself. He had to remind himself that suicide was the sensible thing. He had to put down his hope that something would happen to save him—the death of Hitler, or a last-minute pardon for all political prisoners, or a bombing raid which would destroy the records of his case, or an American parachute attack that would capture Berlin, or the death of Freisler, the chief judge at the People's Court.

There were dozens of such possibilities. New ones kept coming into his mind all the time, but he had to be logical and measure these chances against the certainty of death and the possibility of dragging others down with him. No, he must fight off the hopes that would delay him. Every day in Brandenburg was a gift.

He wrote Hanna a long and careful letter explaining his decision, and a poem called "My Ring, Your Ring." He put his wedding ring with the poem in an envelope, and when that was done he waited for night, took the sleeping pills, cut his wrists as deeply as he could with a razor blade, and lay down to die, committing his family and himself into the hands of God.

> *So nimm den Ring zurück und trag' ihn weiter*
> (Take back the ring, then, and continue to wear it
> *Für mich und denk' dabei, der Ring sei ich:*
> For me, and think the ring were I:
> *Stets Dir verbunden, darum strahlend, heiter,*

Always close to you and therefore gay, serene,
Dich fest umschliessend, schützend ewiglich.
Enclosing and protecting you forever.)

The British bombed Brandenburg around midnight, and the prisoners were taken out of their cells and brought to bomb shelters under the prison. A guard discovered Otto, he was rushed to the hospital, and his life was saved. As a kindness, Thümmler kept him in the hospital longer than he needed to be there. He got out only a few days before his trial.

The trail began at 10 A.M. on July 1, in a courtroom on the first floor of a building on the Bellevuestrasse. There were seats for about a hundred spectators, and the windows were kept open all the time because of the heat. All during the trial, people from the street leaned in the windows and listened.

There were five judges. The chief judge—the President of the Court—was Dr. Roland Freisler, a fanatical and merciless Nazi. He also played the role of prosecutor—shouting, making speeches, turning his head this way and that to express his contempt for those who were before him. "Justice," he liked to say, "is whatever serves the Führer."

Otto, Elisabeth von Thadden, Dr. von Scherpenberg, Irmgard Zarden, Mrs. Solf, and Fanny von Kurowski sat at a single long table facing the judges, all of whom wore the eagle and swastika of National Socialism. Missing was Staatsekretär Zarden, who had committed suicide shortly after his arrest.

The court was full, though not crowded. There were a few women and a number of men, most of whom sat leaning forward with one leg crossed over the other. Being there as spectators was a guarantee that what was happening to the accused wouldn't happen to them. To be able to come and go freely—only showing your identification and signing the list at the door—confirmed that you were on the side of the people in power, who could put cigarettes in your pocket or give you a stamp to buy medicine for your sick old mother.

Dr. Reckzeh was called, and he came forward in his S.S. uniform. He offered no information on his own, so everything he said had to be drawn out of him by the President of the Court. Yes, Dr. Kiep had told the guests at Miss von Thadden's that if a miracle did not occur, the war was lost. Yes, Kiep and Miss von Thadden were the leaders of the conversation, which had included references to the new government after Hitler. Yes, Kiep had given him a card and told him to greet a man named Finkler who lived in Switzerland.

The questions went on, and Freisler became more and more irritated that the witness was making him work for every point. After two hours, Reckzeh was dismissed. He left the room.

The defendants were then examined one by one. Mrs. Solf came first, and she immediately showed her contempt for Freisler by the way she answered his questions. After he had explored the charges against her for a few minutes, her lawyer, Dr. Dix, requested that her case be "separated" from the rest. He showed the President certain papers, and though it was clear that Freisler didn't want to let her out of his hands, he finally agreed to the separation. (It came out later that the Emperor of Japan, remembering her husband's good work in Tokyo, had asked that the esteemed Mrs. Solf be given special treatment.)

Fanny Kurowski came next. She pretended that she didn't completely understand the charge against her or know what "defeatism" was. When Freisler asked her what "form of state" suited her best, she answered in a somewhat dreamy fashion that she wanted the Kaiser back again. Freisler immediately decided that she was probably a little bit crazy and not worth bothering about. He dismissed her and went on to Irmgard Zarden. After half an hour or so, he decided that she too was an unimportant person.

Dr. van Scherpenberg was then questioned at length. He threw himself on Freisler's mercy. Yes, it was true that he had not reported the defeatist remarks of Kiep. Yes, he had kept silent while the courage of German manhood was being put in doubt. No, he could not suggest any defense for himself or anyone else. He trusted that the court would decide his fate justly.

There was a recess, and then Freisler turned his attention to "the chief defendants." Otto was not going to let Freisler make his "crime" bigger than it really was. He admitted what had been reported, but he did not admit more. He didn't lose his temper, but he didn't allow himself to be bullied either. The charges against him were minor. He had spent his life in the service of Germany. He was *not* a traitor, or a fool. As he talked, he could see Freisler's judgment in his eyes, but he refused to let it frighten him. He was a man, and he did not regret what he had done. The questions, broken up by long, shouted speeches, went on for three hours.

Elisabeth von Thadden, who came next, behaved with the same directness, though a few times she went out of her way to admit things that could never have been proven against her.

Otto's father-in-law had hired a well-known lawyer, Dr. Sack, to be Otto's defense attorney. He was an excellent speaker, and it was said that he had friends in high party circles. When it was time for him to speak for his client he stood at the left side of the courtroom so that he could speak to the judges and to the audience in the court at the same time.

He began by pointing out that Otto was only a very recent party member. (He had been sent a party card in 1943, and could not refuse it.) The party, Sack said, had never tried to win over people of Dr. Kiep's generation, and had never expected them to understand the true meaning of National Socialism. Such people deserved to be punished when they acted against the interest of the state, but the punishment should recognize their age and generation.

Dr. Reckzeh, of course, was of the new generation. What, Sack asked, were his motives? Why had he led these older people to make questionable statements? Why had he *urged* them to renew their contacts in Switzerland? Why, when he heard talk which he knew to be defeatist, had he not slammed his fist on the table and put an end to it? Why had he, the only representative of his generation except for Miss Zarden, and the only member of the Nazi elite in the room, why had he not declared himself for victory and the Führer?

Sack spoke for almost twenty minutes, and was brilliant, but it was clear from the beginning that he was angering Freisler by taking attention from him and attacking the witness Freisler had worked so hard to lead. When Sack was through, a recess was declared. The case had been made, and now the President of the Court would prepare his judgment.

In less than an hour Freisler returned and read his decision in a cold and hateful voice.

> At the beginning of the fifth year of war Otto Kiep, in a circle of completely strange countrymen, made highly defeatist remarks about the war situation and tried together with others to make connections with our enemy and to find men who could enter into conversation with the enemy in case of our defeat.
>
> Miss Elisabeth von Thadden played a leading role in this also.
>
> Both have thereby attacked our ability for manly defense and aided our war enemies.
>
> They are forever without honor, and shall be punished by death.

It was over. Otto was taken in a car back to Brandenburg.

Within a week Hanna was released from prison. At first the Gestapo tried to get her to sign a statement that she would not work for her husband's release, but she refused. Finally, when she agreed to sign a paper that she would not discuss her imprisonment, she was brought home. She immediately began to mobilize people to write the Führer and others begging clemency, and to work up materials for appealing the case through legal channels.

That is, she began to do exactly what Otto knew she would do.

On July 20 a bomb went off at Hitler's headquarters. Four people were killed. Hitler was only shaken up. One of the leaders of the plot was Carl Goerdeler. He was captured, and with him a list of men who would serve in the new government. Otto Kiep's name was on that list. He was immediately brought from Brandenburg to the Gestapo prison on the Prince Albrecht Strasse. There he was tortured in terrible ways. Finally he signed a confession, the contents of which he didn't even know, and was transported to the death house at Plötzensee.

A little before noon on August 26 he was taken from his cell and brought to a room where he was given paper and a pen and told that he had thirty minutes to write a last letter. He knew exactly how much he could write in that time. He made notes for ten minutes, and wrote for twenty. He never once looked at the clock on the wall. When the time was up, he was done.

He was brought into the prison yard, where there were five other men also ready for execution. One of them was Adam von Trott zu Solz. They looked at each other but didn't speak. They were led across the yard to the place of execution, a small building where six men could be hanged against the wall at once. The day was clear, the sky a beautiful blue. He did not walk looking down at the ground but with his back straight and his head up. God would care for the rest.

The letter he wrote was never delivered.

Index